THE FIFTH PILLAR
A Spiritual Quest

THE FIFTH PILLAR
A Spiritual Quest

By David Zeidan

OM PUBLISHING
Carlisle, U.K.

Cover design: Mainstream

British Library Cataloguing in Publication Data

Zeidan, David
    Fifth Pillar: Spiritual Pilgrimage
    I. Title
    297.092

    ISBN 1–85078–122–2

OM Publishing is an imprint of Send The Light Ltd,
PO Box 300, Carlisle, Cumbria, CA3 0QS, UK

Typeset by Photoprint, Torquay, Devon
and Printed in Great Britain for
OM Publishing, PO Box 300, Carlisle, Cumbria, CA3 0QS
by Cox and Wyman Ltd, Reading.

Dedication

Nabil, whose story is related here, wishes to dedicate this book to his two sons, in the hope that they will follow him along the true path. He also dedicates it to all his good friends mentioned in this story who helped him along in his spiritual quest.

Contents

Introduction

This is a true story of a spiritual pilgrimage. From the day we are born and until we die we all travel along one path or another in the labyrinth of this world. Some of us seek consciously for guidance and for the true meaning of life – others search for it subconsciously. Some rebel, others submit to what God reveals to them along the path.

Nabil had everything he could wish for – career, money, connections, respectability. Yet something was missing. As he persevered in his spiritual quest, it was finally revealed to him that the ultimate divine truth is not a religious framework of commandments, rituals and traditions, but a Divine Person with whom he could have a personal relationship.

Most names have been changed to protect people from undue exposure.

1

The Quarrel

'Do as you wish,' said Nabil Madani lightheartedly. 'My friends are my own personal affair and you have no right to interfere in my private life.'

Anwar his older brother and Ahmad his boss sat facing him across the coffee table in Nabil's luxury apartment on the eighth floor of a high rise building in the wealthier part of Dubai. They were getting frustrated trying to talk sense into this young man's head. Who did he think he was? How dare he disobey their instructions and keep going his own independent way? It was unthinkable and had to be stopped! They would not budge an inch, and if he didn't submit they would teach him a lesson he would never forget.

'Listen, Nabil,' said Anwar softly, stroking his dark beard, 'this is beyond a joke. You have gone too far down this road and we cannot let you go on like this any further. These are our final conditions,

and you had better accept them: cut off all relationships with Henry and your other western friends and
resume the orthodox Muslim way of life. This is all
we are asking you to do.'

'You have three weeks to decide,' added Ahmad,
'you know we are happy with your work. We only
want your best. You are a Muslim from a respectable
family working for a Muslim publisher – you must
be seen to live as a good Muslim. Surely we are not
asking too much of you – there can be no compromise on this point.'

'I certainly don't need you to tell me what to do,'
retorted Nabil angrily, 'I won't attend prayers with
you any longer seeing you are trying to compel me to
do it. You have no right to force religion down my
throat.'

There followed a heated discussion, but they
wouldn't give in and Nabil countered their offensive
with a determined stubbornness of his own.

'You'd better accept our terms,' they warned him,
'otherwise we'll reject you and see to it that you lose
your job.'

They left his flat in an angry mood. Nabil felt
resentment flowing through him as they walked out.
Just who did they think they were trying to lay down
the law for him in this way? He would show them
that he was a free man able to make his own
independent choices. That snooty brother of his! Just
because he was a year older than Nabil, he thought
he could order him around. It had always been like
this as far back as he could remember. Anwar the

'goody-goody' was always set up as the role model
for Nabil. Nabil the 'regular guy' was never good
enough compared with the shining example of his
older brother. And how bigoted Anwar had become
with his fundamentalist Islamic worldview!

Nabil felt he was as good a Muslim as any, or at
least had been so until quite recently. He had kept
the five pillars of his religion faithfully as well as
most of the traditions – but that didn't mean he
rammed it down other people's throats as these two
were trying to do to him. This was the 20th century
– not the 7th!

A shadow of doubt crept over him as he deliber-
ated. Was he too naïve in his view of the world? He
had always been the spoilt younger son who could
get what he wanted from his doting mother and
sisters and wheedle his way out of any confrontation
with his stern father. He had always assumed that
religion was a man's personal affair – a private
matter between him and God. But was this assump-
tion really true in the world of Islam? He had learned
enough of his religion to realise that Islam demanded
total submission to its dictates in all areas of life –
there was no religious-secular divide, neither was
there a dichotomy between the private and the
communal as far as it was concerned. It was all-
encompassing and claimed God's authority to rule
over every human compartment.

Personal choice was a new fangled western innovation, he suddenly realised. Traditional Sunni Islam
ruled triumphantly and expected total obedience –
this was its God-given duty and needed no apology!

He shuddered as the implications of his meditation impinged on his consciousness. What if they had really meant to implement their threats? What a fool he had been! He should have bent a little, negotiated, compromised – they would have accepted it as a sign of repentance and things could have returned to normal. Why had he been so stubborn? What would they now do?

He went back to his office next day full of apprehension. He was the manager of the Dubai branch of the successful 'Islamic Publishing House' group, founded and owned by Ahmad, his boss. It was a large and prestigious company with branches in all Arabic and most Muslim countries. He had been working for it for over three years now, ever since his brother had introduced him to his friend Ahmad for the first time. Ahmad was looking for the right person to be in charge of his newly established Dubai branch, and Nabil had gladly accepted the job offer with its good pay and career development opportunities.

He had worked hard and Ahmad had been very pleased with him. Nabil had laid down the basics of proper management and accounting procedures, had seen the sales multiply, and saw himself as an up and coming businessman. Everyone had been pleased with his success: his boss, his brother, his colleagues – so what had gone wrong?

The next few weeks were a tense period for Nabil. There was no doubt at all that Ahmad's relationship with him had drastically changed. He ignored Nabil when he saw him in the office, he countermanded his decisions, he disregarded his messages – things couldn't go on like this forever. He made it quite clear that the special relationship he had had with Nabil was now ended.

Weeks passed by and Nabil went on as though nothing had happened. If they thought he would resign, they were very mistaken. He had a signed contract that ran on for several months longer and he had no intention of breaking it. But he was getting worried. What if Ahmad fired him? He still had to stay away from his Syrian homeland for a few more months to finish off the five years abroad required for his exemption from military service. It would be impossible to survive in Dubai without a job, and without a job there was also no visa for the United Arab Emirates of which Dubai was a part. It would be extremely difficult finding another job here if his former boss refused to give him a recommendation. They might even deport him!

Nabil decided to do something about the situation. He contacted the Syrian consul in Dubai and invited him out for dinner. Whilst chatting with the consul he mentioned his father's name and told the consul of his predicament with the several months left to end his five years' period away from Syria.

'Come to my office tomorrow with all your papers,' said the consul helpfully.

Nabil went there the following day, and was given an official document certifying that he had fulfilled his five years out of Syria. It was duly signed by the consul and carried the official stamp of approval. What a relief! Nabil sent it off at once to his father in

Damascus to be passed on to the relevant military authorities. So this problem at least was solved; his father's method of good connections and influence in high places had proven itself once more!

A few weeks later Ahmad came into his office and said: 'Thank you Nabil for your work with our company. I think it is time for you to leave.' He seemed quite cool and relaxed about it.

'You are obliged to give me six weeks' notice,' retorted Nabil, 'I have a signed contract that runs for another four months. What about the outstanding salary? What about compensation? What about my holiday ticket and bonus? After all I've been working here for over three years.'

'Oh, everything will be sorted out,' replied Ahmad suavely, 'I've discussed it all with Anwar. Talk to him and he will arrange for everything.'

Nabil left the office feeling dazed. So they had finally fulfilled their threat. Should he contact Anwar? He decided not to. He would wait till Anwar got in touch with him. In the meantime he returned to his flat and started sorting out and packing his belongings. A couple of days later Anwar phoned to say he was coming around to see him. He arrived at Nabil's flat with his wife. He explained that he himself had initiated the proceedings as Nabil was so stubborn and had refused their offer. It was his fault that he had lost his job.

Nabil felt it would be futile arguing with him. Anwar had made up his mind and there was no going back.

'Can you see to it that I get my outstanding salary

and all payments owed me?' he asked Anwar, 'Ahmad said you would arrange for everything.'

'Oh,' replied Anwar coolly, 'if you want to claim your rights you can take up the matter with the labour court. Ahmad refuses to give you the outstanding payments which are your due.'

Nabil realised that Anwar was being sarcastic. This was all part of the punishment they had devised for him. There was no chance of getting anything through the labour court; the case would drag on for years and would cost a fortune in legal fees. He had calculated that Ahmad still owed him some $15,000 – two months' salaries, holiday money, bonuses, expense accounts – it was a large sum to lose, but there seemed to be nothing he could do about it now.

'Thank you very much for your help,' said Nabil bitterly. 'Would you be so kind as to store some of my belongings in your house?'

Anwar agreed to that. They parted unreconciled. Anwar was angry at his younger brother – how dare he be so independent as to make his own decisions, ignoring him, the elder brother, and the family counsel? It was impudent and inexcusable. He must be chastised and left for a while to stew in his own juice. There was no doubt that he would finally break down, repent and apologise. Nabil must be humiliated and broken – there was no other way of dealing with such a case!

Anwar later arranged for a truck to pass by Nabil's flat and pick up the stuff. Nabil closed down his affairs in Dubai. He left his car with a good friend who promised to sell it and transfer the money

to him wherever he might be. He then packed his
cases, phoned for a taxi to take him to the airport
and boarded a plane headed for Warsaw.

Relaxing in his seat once they were airborne, he let
his mind wander back over the years, recalling his
family's history and the details of his own life. So
much had happened in the few years of his life, but
especially in the last year in Dubai! It was worth
recalling with greater detachment as he left the
turbulent Middle East far behind and headed for the
apparent security and stability of Communist Eastern Europe. He was heading away from all his
troubles, he was free, and he would soon be in
Cracow where Renata was impatiently waiting for
him.

2

In the Mountain of the Druze

Fairouz Madani sat distraught in a wicker chair in a shady corner of the balcony of her house in the small town of Suweida. It was summer, and the sun was beating down mercilessly on the dusty city. She was six months pregnant and was not feeling at all well – had not been feeling well right from the start of this pregnancy. What were they doing here in this God-forsaken corner of southern Syria? If only they had stayed in Damascus, the beautiful capital city with all its amenities, where all their family and friends lived! They had been so happy there during their first year of marriage, until Hasib had been posted to Suweida, capital of the region known as Jebel ad-Druze, as an aide to the Provincial Governor.

Above all Fairouz missed her family. She had always been the centre of the closely knit family circle, her two brothers and three sisters flocking around her for advice, counselling and comfort. She

17

had enjoyed the leadership position that had natur-
ally come her way because of her vivacious and
mature personality. She really loved her family, and
although most of them were now married they still
enjoyed the visits and return visits that were part of
Arabic culture and held the extended families
together. Now it was only once or twice a year that
she was able to return to Damascus for a brief visit
during their annual holidays, and she was very
lonely.

No, it wasn't Hasib's fault. There was nothing he
could do about it. He actually held an important
position, which showed that her husband was highly
respected in the Ministry of Interior. Syria was
reorganising itself in the years after independence,
and needed all available qualified officials to work
hard at maintaining the unity of the new state and at
building up an efficient bureaucracy, especially in the
outlying provinces.

Fairouz was proud of Hasib. Like her, he came
from the respectable, Sunni upper class of Damascus.
His family, originally from Turkey, had been living
in Damascus for two centuries. Her own family had
been living there as far back as anyone could trace it.
It was a great honour to belong to these old families
that had composed the ruling class of Syria ever since
the Muslim conquest in the 7th century. They had
been the backbone of the glorious Umayad Caliphate
that had raised Damascus to the position of capital
of the vast Islamic Empire that stretched from Spain
in the West to India in the East.

In the 1940s Hasib had served as an officer in the

French forces of mandatory Syria and after independence (1946), he was posted to the ministry of interior in Damascus in charge of the project for registering all citizens of the new state and issuing them with identity cards. It was an important job, essential for organising the new state's control over its diverse peoples and for the creation of an efficient tax base. Syria was a hodge-podge of ethnic and religious groups – Sunnis, 'Alawis, Druze, Isma'ilis, Kurds, Turkomans, Christians – it was no easy task to weld them all together into a functioning modern state! Hasib had done well, and in 1954 he was posted to this new position.

Fairouz smiled to herself as she remembered how they had first met – it was really funny. She had been standing at the second floor window of their family house in Damascus eating an apple as she looked out at the busy street scene below. For some reason the apple slipped from her hand and fell down almost on top of a man in uniform who was passing by that very moment. He had looked up angrily and opened his mouth to reprimand the careless culprit, but shut it again in surprise when he saw the beautiful face of this young girl, with her lustrous dark eyes and wavy black hair, looking down at him in shock at what she had done. Their eyes had met, he smiled at her, waved his hand to imply it was nothing, and went on his way. She gazed dreamily after his receding figure, admiring his tall and fair good looks. He was impressive in his neat army uniform and obviously was a high ranking officer she had never met before.

It looked as if he hadn't forgotten her either,

because some days later his mother visited hers to
find out more about their family. It wasn't long
before both his parents visited her own and officially
asked for her hand in marriage to their son.

Hasib later told her that as soon as he got home he
had gone straight to his mother and said: 'I saw a girl
today at this address. Please visit her family – I want
to marry her.' He was a man who acted immediately
and thoroughly once he had made up his mind. It
was one of the traits she so admired in him. His
parents had been looking around at that time for a
suitable girl for him to marry, so when they had duly
checked out her background and found out that
Fairouz came from a respectable family, they were
happy to work out all arrangements and see their son
married to her and settled down.

Marriage arrangements were still made according
to old custom between the parents of the prospective
groom and bride if everything was found to be
suitable. Family was all important – you married
within your social class, or above it if at all possible!
Respectability was a necessity, and both sides spent
some time checking out the other's family background to make sure their own family honour
wouldn't be impaired by this liaison. Money was
important too; power and wealth were interlinked in
the important families of Damascus. Blood is thicker
than water, and once they were joined by marriage
ties, the families were loyal to each other, helping
their members advance socially, economically and
politically, relying on their network of relatives and
of contacts in high places.

She had finally been asked for her consent, and had gladly said 'yes' — at least she had seen him before she was asked and had liked him, which was more than some girls in her position could truthfully claim!

They had been married in 1955 and settled down to the carefree life of the capital city, enjoying life to the full with parties, dancing and visits to friends and family. And then he had been posted to his new position in this distant place amongst the Druze.

The Druze constituted only 3% of Syria's population, but they were a hardy warrior community living in the natural fortresses of their mountainous region near the Jordanian border. In the 1920s they had been the first to rebel against the French colonial power, igniting a fire that had swept on to the nationalist Sunni Arabs of Damascus. The French had retaliated by bombarding the city, and there was fierce fighting before the rebellion had been quelled. Yet Druze loyalty to the new entity called independent Syria was questionable. Some of them had suggested that their area be incorporated into the neighbouring kingdom of Jordan. Being a heretical sect that emerged from Shi'a Islam a thousand years ago, they had been badly treated by the Sunni rulers of Damascus down through the ages, and this grudge could burst out in renewed rebellion unless they were tactfully and firmly treated by the new regime.

Fairouz herself was one of the new generation of Syrian girls that had benefited from further education, and she had trained as a teacher. Independence had brought with it high hopes of education for the masses, and of the fast advance of Syria politically, economically and culturally to become once again the leader of the Arab world. A high rate of illiteracy was inimical to this goal, and the new state was recruiting all its resources to battle against this problem. Here in Suweida she was doing her part to make this dream come true by teaching at the local elementary girls' school.

It was good to have these dreams and feel that you were contributing something to your beloved country. She knew her family and friends did not think her job in Suweida very respectable. For them only a job in the capital city held any prestige. The Damascenes had always looked down on the provincials. Anyway, the fact was that she was very weary and depressed. Their eldest boy, Anwar, had been born just one year before, in 1956, and though he was the pride of her life, she still hadn't regained her strength.

When she found out that she was pregnant again, she wept in despair. She had even tried to terminate the pregnancy by taking some pills the local doctor prescribed for her, but had not succeeded. He had then suggested she take a drive over the very bumpy mountain roads in the area in the hope that it would trigger off a miscarriage, and when that didn't work he sent her to the hot springs at al-Hama in the Yarmuk River valley, but all to no avail. It was getting more and more difficult for her to continue waking up early each morning to trudge to school and stand facing her pupils for hours on end. She needed a break, a rest, a change of scenery.

She did have a Druze maid, Sarah, who came in each day to do the cleaning and cooking and to take care of baby Anwar. A simple country girl, Sarah was devoted to her and to the baby and did her work well. That was one thing about the Druze that Fairouz liked. If you won their loyalty they would stick to you through thick and thin. Sarah had even offered to adopt the unborn child to make things easier for her, but that, of course, was out of the question. A Madani child must be brought up in the strict Sunni Islamic faith of the family. It would be a great shame to give it over to be brought up in the heretical Druze faith. It was unthinkable!

The Druze were basically acceptable. But they were so backward and clannish. The majority of them were still simple peasants, and though they spoke Arabic and were Syrians she had discovered that they had a totally different culture from her own. They appreciated her work for them in education. They respected Hasib's government position. They visited, they brought gifts of their farm produce, but you could not get very close to them. Their secret religion was a barrier that couldn't be crossed. She and Hasib were never invited to attend their prayers or religious activities, and they would never speak of their faith.

As a result of the centuries of persecution, the Druze had retreated into themselves, becoming an introverted religious community that did not seek for converts. All they asked of the outside world was to be left alone to enjoy local autonomy and run their own internal affairs under their designated religious

leaders. They had fought fiercely against all intruders
to preserve their freedom, so they were feared and
respected by the other communities of Syria and
Lebanon.

In November 1957 Fairouz finally gave birth to
another boy. Although there was no hospital at that
time in Suweida, and the child was born at home
attended by a doctor and a midwife, everything went
well and there were no complications. She was so
glad to have another son, so happy to see Hasib's
pride when he first saw the baby. Bearing sons was
honourable. It meant the family name would
continue and not be cut off. They called him Nabil,
and though she was still weak she felt it had all been
worthwhile.

A few months later Hasib brought home the good
news that he was being relocated to Damascus. Her
prayers had been answered and she could now look
forward to settling into her hometown and leading a
fulfilled life there.

3

Damascus, Pearl of the East

In 1958 Hasib and Fairouz with their two boys returned to Damascus. Hasib had been given the important post of Director of the Population Registration Department in the Ministry of Interior, a post he was to hold for thirty years, until his retirement in 1988. It was well paid, he had a government car and chauffeur at his disposal, and most crucial for his career, he was in touch with the really important people in government circles. His future seemed secure.

They settled in a large flat in the modern quarter of Mazra'a. It was near the main Government offices and the diplomatic quarters. In the distance you could see the peaks of the Anti-Lebanon and the summit of the 2,800m high Mt. Hermon, white with eternal snow. The Barada River (the Abana of the Bible) flowing down from the mountains and through Damascus kept it green all year round like an oasis in the desert. All around the city were gardens and orchards, the famous al-Ghutah oasis, criss-crossed by the many channels diverted to irrigate them. It was no wonder that to the ancient Beduin coming out of the barren desert, Damascus and its environs had seemed like a glimpse of Paradise, and tradition had it that this was actually the place of the original Garden of Eden! There is also a Hadith attributed to the Prophet Muhammad that says, 'Blessed is he who owns but the area of a tent stake in Damascus.'

There were wide tree-lined streets in their quarter, and it was within easy walking distance of the old city with its colourful market and famous old buildings. Damascus had so much history! It was considered to be the oldest inhabited city on earth. Egyptians, Hittites, Arameans, Assyrians, Babylonians, Persians, Greeks, Romans, Byzantines, Arabs, Mameluks, Turks, French — all had ruled here for a while at the height of their power. All had left some imprint on the place. But it was the Islamic religion and the Arabic language that had outlived them all and raised Damascus again to be the capital of an independent Arabic Syrian state.

There were the old churches from the Roman and Byzantine periods, and the glorious Great Umayyad Mosque, the earliest surviving stone mosque in the world, built by the Caliph al-Walid I between 705 and 715 AD. Everywhere you went there were memories of ancient days, buildings erected by famous men, tombs of great rulers and of saints. It was no wonder the Damascenes regarded themselves proudly as the élite, not only of Syria, but of the whole Arab world. They looked down scornfully at the 'uncivilised' citizens of the other Syrian towns such as Aleppo, Homs and Hama, as well as at the simple village folk and the wild desert Beduin.

Now that they were close to both sides of the family, there was a lot of mutual visiting and entertaining. Hasib was the eldest brother and as such was recognised as head of the extended family. His brothers and sisters deferred all projects, problems and decisions to him, and his word was final. They showed him much respect, kissed his hand when greeting him and asked for his blessing when leaving. This was the accepted way in Muslim Syrian society which is strongly patriarchal, the eldest male having ultimate authority in the family and clan.

Fairouz had always been the centre of her own family before she married, and her brothers and sisters continued to come to her for counsel and support.

Though they were faithful Sunnis of the Shafi'i school, Hasib and Fairouz weren't very religious. They enjoyed parties, dancing and going out, seeing themselves as modern Muslims who could combine the best of the west with the best in Islam. However, on their return to Damascus they soon fell under the influence of Fairouz's brother, Muhammad, who visited them frequently. Muhammad was a lawyer by profession who had gone on to study Islam under the famous 'Abd al-Krim Rifa'i in the Shari'a university of Damascus, and later at the famous al-Azhar Islamic university in Cairo. He had returned to Damascus as an extremely devout and fanatical Muslim, full of reforming zeal aimed at bringing Islam back to its pristine glory and converting all Muslims to the pure and strict old-fashioned faith.

Muhammad had a charismatic personality and was very convincing. Under his influence, Hasib started visiting the mosque regularly, saying his prayers and keeping all the rituals. Fairouz gave up her teaching in order to devote herself to her home and children as required by traditionalist Islam. Both eventually accepted Muhammad's fundamentalist views as the truth, and firmly believed that this was the right thing to do. Only on one point did Fairouz resist her persuasive brother – she would not wear the traditional veil. He himself was so strict that he would not let any male member of his own family see his wife – only the women and children had access to her.

Being a teacher Fairouz could help train her children from a young age. Both parents had great hopes and plans for them and wanted them to go far in life. At three years of age first Anwar and one year later Nabil were sent to a private Muslim nursery school where they received a good grounding in reading and writing. They had such a good start that when they moved to a regular elementary school at the age of five, they went straight into the second grade.

Later in Damascus three girls were born to the Madanis: Jamileh, Amal and Iman. They were a

closely knit family, and in the security of her beloved
Damascus Fairouz flourished and coped well with
the responsibilities of her growing family. Her health,
however, was never quite restored. It seemed that she
had developed a mild heart condition whilst in
Suweida, but she coped well with all her duties and
was again the centre of her family and acquaint-
ances. This was the world she knew and loved and it
was wonderful having relatives and friends all living
near by.

Religion gave them stability and a sense of
belonging to the great Islamic nation (the 'Ummah'),
whilst Hasib's job made them part of the upper class
of Syrian society. They had all they could desire.
They were looked up to and respected by their
neighbours. They were 'in'.

Hasib was a stern father. He believed in the old-
fashioned virtues coupled with military discipline.
Obedience was expected and enforced. When he had
decided on something, no cajoling could ever make
him change his mind! You didn't joke with your
father or treat him as a friend! Oh no! The children
had to treat both parents with due respect and
decorum. They kissed their father's hand when
greeting him and looked at the floor when speaking
to him. They were not allowed to sit with their
parent's visitors unless specifically asked to join
them. They had to ask for their parents' blessing
every time they met them. This was what Islam
taught. Respecting your parents and obeying them
was equivalent to respecting and obeying God
himself. As it is written: 'You will not even say

"uffa" to them' (meaning you will never answer back in any way).

Hasib really organised the children's life for them. Every minute had to be accounted for. Each child received a weekly allowance, and it was no use begging for more if you had spent it all in the first days. Not a cent was forthcoming until the next pay day.

Family ties were very strong in the Madani household. Their social life now revolved mainly around the extended families of both sides, with much cross visiting and entertaining. The former worldly pleasures were shunned and forbidden to the growing children. The family and the mosque were now seen as being the natural centres and shelters of the devout.

Fairouz spent much time coaching the children with their homework, and Hasib would check on their work and on how they had spent their time. The children were given all they needed. Each boy had his own private corner, with his own desk, chair and shelves, where he could study and do his homework without being disturbed. This stress on education brought results. They did very well indeed at school, Anwar especially distinguishing himself as a brilliant scholar. Nabil too was always at the top of his class, elected to be the teacher's special aide in arranging the chairs, cleaning the blackboard and checking for absent students. This position was considered to be a special privilege. He was also the one called upon to give a speech on behalf of the pupils on Mothers' Day.

Having decided to turn to religion, Hasib, as was his nature, went the whole way. He would go five times a day to the mosque to perform his prayers (salat), not just to the dawn and sunset ceremonies commanded by Muhammad, but at all five times accepted by tradition. He saw to it that all members of the family kept strictly to the prescribed prayer times. If they were at home and for some reason unable to go to the mosque, he would gather them all, even at 4 o'clock in the morning, for the dawn prayer. He would stand in front, the two boys behind him, and Fairouz and the girls in the back row, all facing Mecca and devoutly repeating the familiar formulas and prostrating themselves before God.

The Ramadan fast was strictly kept in the Madani household. Fairouz would get up early in the morning, before the sun had risen, to prepare 'S'hur', the early breakfast. Everyone got up before dawn and they ate together. Then, as soon as the muezzin called with the rising of the sun, everyone, including the children would fast from food and drink until after sunset when they broke the fast together as a family. They would pray together, standing in rows behind Hasib, then go to the mosque where the special prayer had to be repeated twenty times.

According to Islamic law children are supposed to start fasting from the age of seven. Between seven and nine they can break the fast earlier than adults, but from nine years onwards they must fast the whole day or be beaten! Hasib awarded some money to those who completed the fast — the children would often cheat, have a quick bite and sip of water in the bathroom, and then swear they never had a morsel the whole day and so pocket the prize. It was especially tough when Ramadan fell in the summer time, with the intense heat. Smokers seemed especially affected, and one uncle, a heavy smoker, would often lose his temper and start swearing and cursing about the necessity of fasting. People would say: 'How dare you use such language in Ramadan? It is better if you eat and shut up!'

At the end of Ramadan came the three day feast of 'Id al-Fitr. The children were off school for this holiday. In preparation for the feast, they were entitled to accompany their parents to the market and choose a new set of clothes and shoes for themselves. Adults who visited had to give them a gift of money – the children all competed with each other as to who would collect most. Invariably it was Anwar, as the gifts would be given according to age – Anwar got most, followed by Nabil and then the girls. Nabil was always upset that he couldn't catch up with his older brother. He needed the money just as much as Anwar – it wasn't fair! The money usually lasted for quite a while, being used for daily purchases of chocolate and sweets at school.

Fairouz would be busy in the kitchen for days before the feast, preparing large quantities of food and the delicious special cakes for the occasion called Ma'moul – she would bake three to four hundred of them! Every visitor had to eat something before he left.

Hasib, Fairouz and the children would also dutifully visit grandparents, uncles and aunts. Everyone visited everyone else in honour of this feast.

On return to school, there were many stories to tell and comparisons to be made about what each one had received for the feast.

Another important aspect of this feast was the giving of special alms to the poor, called zakat al-Fitr. Hasib had to pay a certain amount for each member of his family and distribute it to needy families. He would sit with Fairouz and draw up a list of those who needed it most this time – it had to be in their hands before the first day of the feast.

'Id al-Adha, the four day feast at the end of the Pilgrimage was another important festival to which the children looked forward. There was a school holiday, and again the adults had to provide new clothes and money gifts – it was like having two Christmases each year!

Hasib would ask an uncle to buy a sheep for the family, and the butcher would come around to their block to carry out the ritual slaughter of the sacrificial sheep for all who wanted it. Hasib read a few verses from the Qur'an, the slaughterer said Bism'illah ('in the Name of God') and cut its throat in the street letting all the blood flow out. The women and children would watch from the balconies. Later they would go down to wash their street clean. The butcher would skin the sheep and cut it up for the family – Fairouz would keep ten per cent of the best cuts to cook for themselves, and the rest had to be wrapped up in neat packages and distributed to several needy families in the area.

Anwar and Nabil had the job of distributing the packages.

It was important to keep exactly to all religious rituals and to perform good deeds like giving to the poor. This would greatly increase your chances of getting into Paradise when the terrible Day of Judgement arrived, and your good deeds would be balanced against your bad ones. Everything was written down, everything was remembered, and it was best to increase your store of good deeds and of merit as much as possible while you still had the chance.

Muhammad's Birthday — Mawlad al-Nabawwi — was also celebrated in a big way. Every mosque would set out chairs in the street and string up special lights and green banners with verses glorifying the prophet. The radio and TV stations would broadcast the service from the great mosque in Damascus attended by the president himself. In the afternoon everyone went to his local mosque for the special service of chanting and prayers. Later the mosque would distribute a small bag of sweets wrapped in cellophane to all comers.

The religious feasts were celebrated at home and in the mosque. At school they celebrated the national feasts — especially independence day on July 17th and Revolution Day on the 8th of March. The classrooms would be decorated and there would be speeches and recitals of poems glorifying the state and its leaders. For Nabil the enjoyable part was that there were no classes, no lessons and no homework!

4

Growing up with Islam

Hasib attended some religious instruction classes at the mosque, but, unlike Muhammad, did not feel called to immerse himself in the vast sea of Islamic theology. Muhammad eventually got into trouble with the authorities because of his activities with the Muslim Brotherhood. During the rule of Nur al-Din Attassi, the government ordered a crackdown on the brotherhood, and suspicion fell on Muhammad too. The police were looking for him, and Hasib came to his help by hiding him in his house for a few days and then helping him to get out of the country and fly to Saudi Arabia. There he eventually got a job in the Saudi ministry of education and settled in Medina.

After school hours, the boys were sent to attend an Islamics course at the Zayd Mosque in the old city. It served as an Islamic centre, with schools for all age groups and it also contained conference facilities.

Even in the summer holidays they were made to
attend these classes – they certainly didn't always feel
like it, but never dared to disobey their father. At the
best they could sometimes escape for an hour or two
with other boys to play in the nearby streets. The
teacher would report them to their fathers, and they
would get a scolding or a tug on the ear for their
frivolity.

Day after day from 4 to 8 pm Anwar and Nabil
had to trudge to the mosque and memorise passages
from the Qur'an, study the Hadith, the Sunnah and
Fiqh. Anwar seemed to enjoy these studies much
more than Nabil, and was much admired by all for
his religious zeal and learning. Nabil found it all
rather boring, but did what was required of him. He
was especially zealous in memorising the Qur'an –
Hasib paid 35 Syrian cents for every page memor-
ised! Eventually he came to know at least three-
quarters of the Qur'an by heart.

Hasib kept investigating the Damascus schools to
make sure his boys attended only the very best. This
meant they had to change schools several times, and
Hasib used his government position and connections
to get the necessary authorisation for these changes
which were not available to ordinary citizens.

Nabil enjoyed sports. He was involved in basket-
ball, football and volleyball. He also liked Arabic
and maths, but he could never keep up with his older
brother who was considered to be a model child.
Anwar was diligent and pious, and though he loved
him, Nabil thought he was becoming something of a
prig. He couldn't share his deeper secrets with

Anwar and had to make his own friends at school who understood him and shared his boyish interests. Hasib also registered them both in the local library and made sure they read good books – they had to brief him regularly about what they had read.

The Madani boys weren't allowed to play at school or on the streets after school hours like other children. They weren't allowed to walk around the streets with their friends or even visit them in their homes without explicit permission. Hasib wanted to know who these friends were, and made sure they kept only the very best company – boys from respectable, well-off Sunni families. They could go out only if accompanied by their parents.

They were forbidden to visit Christian boys or invite them home. Christians were considered impure, eaters of pork and drinkers of alcohol, worshippers of three Gods, guilty of the worst possible sin – that of 'Shirk', of joining a man to God, thus giving the Almighty a partner. Christians were also the proprietors of the shady night spots of Damascus – immoral bars, night clubs and discotheques which no reputable Muslim would ever frequent.

Hasib's chauffeur, supplied by the Ministry, was a Christian named Joseph. They had a working relationship, but no social contact. He seemed to live up to their stereotype of the immoral Christian who was interested only in where he could buy the cheapest drinks, or which cabaret he should visit that night. His wife even went out alone with one of his friends – an unthinkable act for a devout Muslim woman.

In Junior High Nabil was very friendly with a

Christian boy called Raymond. One day he invited him to visit the Madani home, and then belatedly asked Fairouz's permission.

'What is his name?' she asked.

'Raymond,' replied Nabil.

'He is a Christian,' she concluded (the name gave him away), 'I won't allow him to enter this house.'

'Why?' persisted Nabil stubbornly. His only answer was a slap across the face for daring to question parental authority. For the next few days he had to invent various excuses as to why it was inconvenient for Raymond to visit their home, until the matter faded away.

So the boys grew up in a very protected environment, circumscribed by religion and family ties. Nabil especially resented this extreme strictness, and often felt ashamed in front of his freer living peers, but there was nothing he could do about it. He also battled with feelings of jealousy towards Anwar, who as well as enjoying the privileges of the eldest child was the favourite son. Whether it was furniture, clothes, bicycles, or anything else, Anwar always got them brand new whilst Nabil had to be content with his brother's discarded belongings. It really wasn't fair being the second!

Hasib could have advanced his career very fast had he not turned to fundamentalist Islam. The Ba'ath party was in the ascendancy, and most government officials joined the party in order to further their careers. Hasib was invited to join, but refused. He liked their development policies and their militant anti-Israel stance, but he couldn't accept their antireligious ideology. For that reason he had to watch on the sidelines as some of his friends advanced to ministerial positions whilst he stayed in the very same post for many years. It was frustrating, but he was a man of principle and wouldn't give in. As a Sunni, he was also galled by the ascendancy of the 'Alawis into all influential positions especially with the installment of Hafiz Assad as president.

It was the curse of Syria, he thought, to have so many small splinter communities living within its borders. The Sunnis composed over sixty percent of the population and had always been the ruling class, but Syria was a mixture of many religious and ethnic minority groups, each leading its own separate communal life. You were what you were born into. There could be no intermarriage or change of identity. You were loyal first and foremost to your own community. Pan-Syrian nationalism was a modern innovation that could be tolerated as long as it didn't run counter to the deep set traditional loyalties.

The 'Alawis, the Druze and the Isma'ilis had all emerged from the ancient Shi'a groups of Islam who revered 'Ali and his descendants as semi-divine figures, a belief abhorrent to all rightly believing Sunnis. The 'Alawis were the largest minority group, comprising 13% of the total population. They lived mainly in the northwest region of Syria called Jebel al-Ansariya and had been cruelly persecuted as heretics by the Sunnis over centuries. This then was their hour of revenge.

South of the 'Alawis lived the Isma'ilis, a much

smaller community whose ancestors had at one time almost gained control of the whole Muslim world. During the period of the Crusades they had been notorious as the sect of the Assassins led by the 'Old Man Of The Mountain', and all Middle East rulers, Muslims and Christians alike, had lived in fear of their daggers.

The Kurds, comprising another 10% of the Syrian population lived mainly in the northeast. Though Sunni Muslims, they were not Arabs, but spoke their own Kurdish language and kept their own ancient tribal culture. They were kept under constant tight supervision by the security forces because of their desire for autonomy.

There were also the Turkomans, Turkish-speaking splinters of tribes that had one time swept into Anatolia from Central Asia and had won it from the Byzantine Christians.

The Christian communities in Syria composed another 10% of the population, most of them descended from the ancient inhabitants of Syria who had dwelt there from time immemorial. They had been Christianised during the Roman period and split into rival churches during the Byzantine era. Persecuted by the official Greek Orthodox state church, the Aramaic (Syriac) speaking Jacobite and Nestorian churches had welcomed the Muslim conquerors as liberators. They still retained their old rituals and used Aramaic as their liturgical language.

Ruling this unusual mixture of ethnic and religious groups needed a very delicate balancing act by the central government!

For Nabil, high school was an exciting time. He was now a little more independent of his parents, and could spend more time with his school friends, studying with them after school hours, preparing for exams or working on projects. He felt his personality developing in response to the new stimuli. For the first time he met the outside world and encountered other ways of thinking and of looking at life.

Actually he attended three different high schools in Damascus, due to Hasib's preoccupation with getting only the very best for his children. The last one was the famous Jawdat al-Hashemi school, housed in the imposing building of the former parliament during the French mandate and named after a Syrian national hero. It was a first class school, attended mainly by children of the best families in Damascus: high government officials, diplomats, army officers and the richest businessmen. Some pupils were dropped off by shining Mercedes limousines or sporty Porsches every morning – luxurious status symbols. Nabil was ashamed of his father's drab ministerial car and would ask Joseph to drop him off some distance from the school so that his friends wouldn't see the vehicle he was brought in.

With other boys from his class he would sometimes play truant and go into the town centre to loaf around or visit a cinema. When discovered, they would be brought before the headmaster who demanded that their fathers come to see him. That was a standing joke, as most of these fathers, including Nabil's, had such a high position that the teachers and the headmaster were afraid of doing anything to their precious offspring.

Life still revolved around Islam. Nabil had to keep all the rituals, his parents enforcing them as a duty to God. Hasib would ask him every evening: 'Did you say your prayers at the appointed times?' Even if he had missed them, Nabil was so afraid of the punishment meted out that he always answered in the affirmative. Sometimes, if Hasib was suspicious, Nabil would have to prove his statement and often recruited one of his sisters as a false witness to the fact that he had faithfully performed his religious duties. Amal was his favourite sister and she would often support him when he faced trouble.

Lying became the way out of these difficult situations and he had to invent excuses by the dozen to get through the cross-examinations. Gradually religion came to be seen as a burdensome ritual that had to be observed out of fear of the consequences. Honesty didn't pay, because there was no forgiveness for any infringement, and the punishment was severe. Deception got you out of your problems. This distortion marred what had once been a happy family life.

There were a few Christian pupils in his class, and Nabil became friendly with Edmund, whose father had a high government position, so that Hasib could not forbid Nabil's visiting him. He would sometimes go to Edmund's home after school to study with him. Edmund's family would invite him to stay and have a meal with them and he sometimes accepted. He noticed that these Christians, whom he had been taught to despise, had an easier relationship with their parents and their religion. It was not dominated by fear, but by honesty and trust. They felt free to tell their parents the truth about where they had been and what they had done. They attended their Church not because they were compelled to do so, but because they wanted to. This gave Nabil food for thought. What made the difference?

Anwar had quite a different experience at high school. He joined the Muslim Union and would regularly attend prayer and Qur'anic instruction. Hasib noticed the difference between his two sons, and would often scold Nabil: 'You have the wrong set of friends and they have a bad influence on you. Keep away from them. Try to be like your brother – he has the right kind of friends and I can trust him to perform his religious duties. I don't have to ask him where he's been or what he's done – I know he's okay.' This gave Nabil an inferiority complex. Why was Anwar so much better than he was? Why was he always the good boy, whilst Nabil was the black sheep of the family? It just wasn't fair!

In spite of these problems, Nabil did fairly well at school and graduated with good grades – but not good enough for Hasib! Anwar had graduated top of his class and started studying civil engineering at Damascus University. Hasib had hoped Nabil would do the same – engineering was at that time considered the most prestigious subject to study in Syrian universities. You needed top grades to be accepted in the engineering faculties; you had to be a real genius. The government was in great need of these graduates, so they received the highest salaries and were very respected. Nabil's grades however weren't high enough for engineering. As usual, a family council was called to discuss the matter.

Nabil suggested he go abroad and study in the United States or Britain, as some of his friends were planning to do, but Hasib and Fairouz were completely against it. The decadent west would have a bad influence on him and he would be totally out of their control. It was finally decided that he should register at Damascus University for Accountancy studies.

Military service was deferred for students until the end of their course, so Anwar and Nabil were free to enjoy their student years.

Anwar, as usual, did very well at University. He got the highest grades and won several medals. He was also very involved with Muslim student groups, and, unknown to his father, became a member of the extreme Muslim Brotherhood. Nabil on the other hand made friends with more 'normal' students. They enjoyed going out together to parties, dancing, discos and picnics. Studies were alright, but life was to be enjoyed – and what better time to enjoy life than in your student days?

Hasib and Fairouz were worried about their younger son. He wasn't taking his religion seriously enough, and something had to be done about it. They warned Nabil of the dangers of hell fire and exhorted him to pray and study the Qur'an regularly. They reminded him that there was no forgiveness for sins of omission or commission – the only possibility was to compensate by doing good deeds that would tip the balance in your favour. The two angels were busy registering all his bad deeds and all his good ones, and only on the final day of judgement would the result be known. He'd better do his best now, or it would be too late!

They set up Anwar as an example and said that he did so well because he wisely chose the right set of friends. They reminded Nabil of his piety as a child and of the fact that he had learnt almost the whole Qur'an by heart. Why had he changed? Couldn't he simply follow their example and be content?

Finally, towards the end of his first year at university, they had another family council to discuss what to do with Nabil. Parents, elder brother and stern uncle on a visit from Saudi Arabia, all gathered together to find a way out. Muhammad, his fanatically religious uncle, finally had an inspiration: Send the boy on the pilgrimage (Haj) to Mecca! Surely this highest of all religious duties and experiences would purify his soul from all attachment to worldly pleasures. God would work there in his heart and change him to become like his brother and uncle. According to tradition once you've been on the Haj you're a new born man – all your sins are washed away. Their goal was to see him stop wearing jeans, start growing a beard, and be a perfect Muslim keeping all the traditions and commandments. They would give anything to see it happen.

Nabil resisted the idea with all his might. He was only nineteen years old and the Haj was for old men! It was supposed to atone for the sins of a lifetime –

so why not wait until he was fifty years old and had accumulated a respectable burden of sins – that would make the Haj worthwhile and expiate all his sins! His friends would laugh at him if he went now. Anyway, he was a good enough Muslim. He believed in the One God and in his Prophet. He prayed regularly and gave alms to the poor. He fasted during Ramadan – what more did they want of him?

They would not listen to him and went on with their plans. The arrangements were made and the tickets bought, leaving him no option. His friends at University joked and laughed about it. What a young Haji! It was embarrassing, but there was no way out. So finally one bright day in the autumn of 1976 he was driven to the assembly point for the pilgrimage, given his money and documents and accompanied to the bus that would take him all the way to the holy city of Mecca.

5

The Haj

Nabil left Damascus for Mecca in a convoy of six buses especially organised for Syrians going on the pilgrimage. It was autumn and they travelled overland, taking the ancient route via Amman and Ma'an in Jordan, on to Tabouk in Saudi Arabia and then on to Mecca via Medina.

The convoy was well organised: there were water tanks in every bus, a leader took care of any problems, the convoy was attended by a medical team of doctor and nurse, an ambulance was part of the convoy and there was a special truck for their luggage.

This was part of the large movement of Syrians into Mecca for the annual Haj — it followed the tradition and experience of 1,300 years of sending camel caravans of pilgrims annually from Damascus. It had always been the responsibility of the ruler of Damascus to organise the caravans from his city, which was the assembly point for Muslims from all over Syria, Iraq, Iran and even farther East. This was part of the privilege of belonging to the worldwide Umma (nation) of Islam, expressed by millions of pilgrims from almost every country in the world converging on the Holy City to fulfil this Pillar of their Faith.

They drove through the vast featureless desert spaces, and arrived in Mecca on the fourth day. The pilgrims were very excited. They had finally arrived at Mecca 'the blessed', the 'Mother of Cities', the centre of the Muslim world! It was a very emotional experience. Some of them had been saving over a lifetime for this privilege.

Their group was allocated rented flats in a building quite near to the Sacred Mosque. There they could freshen up, don the special white garment (Ihram) worn by all pilgrims, and then follow their guide into the great mosque to comply with the first duty: going seven times around the Ka'abah — the venerable shrine at the centre of the mosque and at the centre of Muslim piety.

Nabil didn't change into the compulsory white garment but went dressed in jeans and T-shirt. Hasib had told him to buy the right garment immediately on arrival in Mecca, but he didn't. He assumed he could do it later. It was a childish act of rebellion, of trying to be different, of saying: 'What does it really matter?' His companions weren't pleased with him, they were rather shocked! On his first sighting of the Ka'abah he stopped to pray and utter a personal wish, for his mother had assured him that a wish uttered at this first sighting of the holy place was sure to be granted by God! He had avoided looking out of the bus window as they neared the town centre in order to make sure he didn't lose the chance of being granted this special wish.

Entering the great mosque, which can accommodate 300,000 people, at one of the many gates supervised by special guards, he was spotted and received a blow on his head from the guard's truncheon. He was ordered to go out and return dressed in the white Ihram garment. Instead of obeying, he went out and slipped in through another gate where the guards didn't notice him amongst the crowds surging by. He had lost his group, but it was no use looking for them in the masses of people surging around the Ka'abah in the central open plaza. The only thing to do was to perform the ceremonies on his own and then find the others at their appointed meeting place outside the mosque.

Now that he was inside the holiest shrine of Islam he felt elated. After all this was God's House, the place Abraham was commanded to erect. He felt himself in the presence of a holy and all-powerful deity.

Seven times he went around the shrine, at one with the masses around him, all walking in an anti-clockwise direction around the holy Ka'abah, all reciting Qur'anic verses and calling out the special prayer of submission to God for this occasion:

'Labbayka, Allahumma, Labbayka. Labbayka, la sharika lak. Labbayka, inna al-hamda wal-ni'imata lak, wal-mulk! ...' ('At your service, my God, at your service. You have no partner, yours the praise and the grace and the kingdom!')

It was a moving experience. All pilgrims want to get near the shrine so they can touch it and kiss it. This earns you special merit and forgiveness. If you can but kiss the Black Stone your body will never touch hell fire even if the angels try to throw you into it! It was difficult and dangerous to force your way into the inner circle nearest the shrine. Every year some people were trampled to death by the marching crowds who couldn't stop for anyone because of the pressure from those behind them. The nearer you got to the centre, the more you were pushed and jostled.

Some African pilgrims had perfected a special technique to enable them to touch the shrine. They would form a circle with their strongest men outside and the women and children inside. The outside ring would link hands and advance swinging their hands powerfully up and down in rhythm with their prayers. Woe to any one who tried to push through their group and got hit by these powerful arms — if he fell down, there was little chance of his ever getting up again!

Some pilgrims had brought their coffins with them, and paid for them to be washed in the water of the holy Zemzem well and then placed for a few moments touching the wall of the Ka'abah. They then took them back home and asked their families to make sure they were buried in these coffins when they died. This would protect them from hell forever.

The guide had given the whole group some good

advice before going in: 'Don't take any cash or valuables in with you; there are always pickpockets busy in the crowd! If you see someone falling down – don't bend down or kneel to help them – it may be the last thing you do! Just keep moving on, it's the guards' duty to try and save them.'

Nabil did succeed in finally reaching and touching the wall of the Ka'abah and its heavily embroidered silk covering (the Kiswa; a new one is brought each year by pilgrims from Egypt), but he couldn't get near the Black Stone itself which was placed there by Adam. He finished the seven rounds quite pleased with himself. He then went on to the nearby spot where Abraham was supposed to have prayed – it is clearly marked – and said some prayers there. This again earns you some merit for the day of judgement. Then he stopped by the holy Zemzem well to drink of the hallowed water and say a prayer.

Next he went to Safa' and Marwa, the two hills between which Hagar had run seven times searching for water when Abraham left her in the desert with Ishmael. The distance between the two spots is half a mile, and Nabil walked and ran between them seven times as prescribed. All these holy places are in the enclosed area of the great mosque – a huge covered area of marble and stone, very impressive and in our modern times even air-conditioned! This finished the first day's duties and he returned to his room.

They stayed as was the custom two more days in Mecca. It was very hot, and Nabil found the water unpalatable – so he stuck to Pepsi and Cola. Some families invited him to share their meals with true

Arab hospitality. Five times a day they would all crowd to the mosque for the prayer ceremonies.

On the fourth day after arrival they were taken by bus to Mina, some miles out of Mecca, where all the pilgrims camp for two days preparing for the main part of the Haj. A huge camp was erected there, divided into sections by countries and sub-groups from within the countries. The flag of each state flew on a pole at the centre of each subdivision so that you could find your way. Their group was taken to their special corner of the Syrian camp, where they met many other Syrian pilgrims. The leader of the mosque in Nabil's neighbourhood happened to be there and he was pleased to see Nabil and took him under his wing (later, in 1984 he had to flee Syria for Saudi Arabia because of his involvement with the Muslim Brotherhood). These two days were spent reciting the Qur'an, praying and listening to preachers.

From this camp, on the ninth day of the Muslim pilgrimage month Dhu al-Hijjah, after shaving off some of his hair and cutting his fingernails, Nabil changed into a clean white garment that left his right shoulder bare and walked a distance of three miles to the place where Abraham and Muhammad defeated the devil. There he threw stones at a pillar representing Shaitan, Satan (and made sure he didn't get hit by stones being thrown with great force by other pilgrims). From there he moved on with the teeming crowds to Mount 'Arafat, the Mount of Mercy. The duties of this day are the centre of the pilgrimage. They are the ones laid down in the Qur'an as obligatory – every thing else is the tradition of the Sunnah. Some people fly out to Mecca only for this one day to fulfil their pilgrimage duties if they don't have the time for the full period. Anyone who has completed these rites is entitled to the title 'Haj' and is highly respected on his return home.

From 'Arafat it was back to the camp – full with hundreds of thousands of people from every corner of the Muslim world, now that all the pilgrims were concentrated in this one place. The remainder of this day was again spent in reciting prayers and listening to preachers. This is a very holy time. Nabil was quite shocked when he realised the preacher was talking politics rather than religion, criticising their own Syrian government for not being Muslim enough. The man became very excited, and it affected his audience, some of whom became hysterical. Women screamed and wept and one men fainted and had to be taken away for medical treatment. This really bothered Nabil who thought it was in bad taste and a wholly unfitting end to this most holy day.

It was very sunny that afternoon with not a cloud in the sky. Suddenly a cloud appeared from nowhere and there was a downpour of rain! It was very unusual for that time of the year near Mecca. People said it was a sign from God showing his mercy and approval of the Haj. Later, on their return to Damascus, it was still a main news item and theme of gossip – God's special sign at the Haj.

They then returned to Mecca, where they again went seven times around the Ka'abah and ran seven

times between Safa' and Marwa. People around him
were weeping with emotion and feeling God's special
grace and presence — but this time Nabil felt no joy,
no peace, no special emotion. It was a duty that had
to be carried out and he performed it as such, but
there was no response in his heart to the frenzy of the
crowds.

Then the Haj was over with — he had performed it
all! He was now officially a Haji! He would be called
Haj Nabil Madani — it was a strange feeling.

Next day they all returned to Mina for the four
day 'Id al-Adha (feast of sacrifice) ceremonies that
mark the end of the Haj period. Nabil bought a
sheep at the market and hired someone to slaughter
it for him ritually as required for the sacrifice. He
could eat only a small portion of the meat, the
remainder was supposed to be given to the poor, but
everyone around had their own sheep and were
roasting it and eating happily of it. He mused on the
waste of good meat that couldn't be kept as it would
quickly spoil in that hot climate. So much had to be
simply thrown away.

On the following day he joined part of his group
who were going to Medina, the second holiest city of
Islam, whilst the others headed back to Damascus.
They drove the 425 kilometres in their aircondi-
tioned bus and on arrival they were again put up in
rented flats in the city centre near to the Mosque of
the Prophet (Masjad ash-Sharif) that holds Muhammad's tomb. After refreshing himself in his room,
Nabil went down to meet his Uncle Muhammad who
lived in Medina and had come to pick him up. His

uncle took him to see Muhammad's tomb in the centre of the green-domed mosque – it was a huge mosque and could easily hold a quarter of a million people.

There is a special ritual (the Ziyyarah) for this visit, starting at the Gate of Peace and reciting special prayers at specified points. It was a touching experience for Nabil. Having heard all his life of the great prophet for whose sake, according to tradition, God had created the world, it was exciting to be actually in the city of the Hejirah and at his very tomb! It made everything seem so real. People sat beside the tomb reciting the Qur'an – some would sit there for two or three days to recite the whole book over and over again. Masses of people were again pushing their way to be able to touch the tomb that was covered by a golden curtain. Women wept, men threw money on the floor beside it. If you could but touch the tomb, all your sins would be forgiven!

Next to Muhammad's tomb were the tombs of the first two of the 'rightly guided' Caliphs – Abu-Bakr and 'Umar, considered to be the most excellent of the Muslim community after Muhammad himself. They prayed beside these tombs and then went out for some lunch in town. Uncle Muhammad was very hospitable and generous. Nabil stayed in his house where he was treated as an honoured guest. He couldn't see his aunt – she only spoke to him through a closed door, welcoming him, asking about the family in Syria and sending her greetings to them. His uncle was indeed very strict in his religious observance. Nabil had to accompany him five times a

day to the mosque for prayers; it became boring and
tedious over the four weeks he spent there. There
were some compensations as his uncle took him
sightseeing in and around Medina. He liked this city;
it was an oasis and had many trees and there was
water to be seen. Mecca was dry and bare in
contrast. They went on some picnics, did some
shopping, visited the school where his uncle taught
and the mosque Muhammad had built on his arrival
in this city.

Muhammad would have liked to have kept Nabil
in Medina – he offered to arrange for him to study in
the main Saudi Shari'a university and to see that he
got a special visa for it. But Nabil wouldn't hear of
it. He was eager to leave the oppressive and stifling
religious atmosphere of Saudi Arabia and of his
uncle's home, and return to the relative freedom of
Damascus University and his easy-going friends.

Saudi Arabia was unbearably hot at this time of
the year and Nabil suffered greatly from the heat.
The Saudi people were very different from the
Syrians. After all they were mainly Beduins, some of
whom had only recently settled in the towns – there
was no sophisticated bourgeoisie as there was in
Syria. Even the richest of them were still rough desert
nomads at heart and in behaviour, steeped in the
ideas of extreme Wahabi Islam. Nabil was impressed
by the size of the country – the great Arabian
peninsula – and by the obvious efforts at development and modernisation made by the authorities.
Some of the oil wealth was clearly being invested for
the benefit of the country as a whole. This was

visible in the good roads and the new buildings. On the other hand, in spite of their oil wealth, the Saudis still seemed bent on getting all they could from the pilgrims. You had to pay for your visa, for the official guides, for the entrance to the holy sites, for the sacrifices – and a good part of these many fees went to the Saudi authorities.

It was a relief to have finally done it all. After some forty days spent in Saudi Arabia he was free to return to Syria and to his friends at university. Nabil was a celebrity on his return, family and friends crowded to see him, hug him, touch him, get a share of the special blessing (baraka) attached to a Haji. He was supposed to be a new creation, without sin, an unwritten slate like a newborn baby, fresh and clean. For three days he just sat at home whilst visitors came and went, and he had to tell them all about the Haj. They all said they wished they could have gone too. He was a hero – but he didn't enjoy all this attention!

He was expected to bring back some mementos from the pilgrimage for the family – dates from the holy city, holy Zemzem water, some holy sand – but he hadn't bothered about it and his mother was disappointed.

When he returned to university he was embarrassed as his friends joked about his pilgrimage and called him a 'holy man', a 'Haji'.

'Give us your blessing, Haj Nabil,' they would say, 'let us touch you and partake of your grace.'

It took a while for the excitement to die down. His parents watched him carefully to see if he had indeed changed. They soon noticed that the holy Haj hadn't made much difference to Nabil. Fairouz especially was very worried and spent much time talking to him about the importance of having the right attitude towards God and the religious require-ments of Islam. She encouraged him not to neglect his prayers, to visit the mosque, read the Qur'an and be a pious Muslim.

'Nabil,' she would say, 'I hear the muezzin calling. Aren't you joining your father to go to the mosque for prayers?'

'Oh, I've just got to finish something I've started doing,' he would answer, 'I'll follow him to the mosque in a few moments.'

He didn't go. Later he would invent excuses. He was too busy with his studies, so he had prayed alone in his room. There were many arguments and disagreements. He got into the habit of deceiving his parents in order to escape from their constant pressure.

The religious duties he was still performing weren't good enough for them. To be a really good Muslim he had to go much further – he ought to grow a beard, become a pupil of some famous Sheikh, study his Sunni Shafi'i school of thought, traditions and commentaries.

Nabil was really upset. He had always thought of himself as a good Muslim – he believed, he prayed, he fasted, he gave to the poor, he had even gone on the Haj – what more could they want? But it wasn't good enough for them! It was really frustrating and made him very angry. Why wouldn't they leave him alone? They couldn't force him into anything he didn't want to do! He would keep to the basic rituals if they left him alone – but if they continued applying pressure and checking on him continually he would let it all go. Religion ought to be a personal matter – who did they think they were to keep pestering him? He got into the habit of going his own way and inventing little deceptions and excuses to keep them at bay.

6

University Days

Nabil settled back happily into the university world
with his assorted friends. The best one was Kamal
who like him came from a good Sunni family and
had been with him right through elementary and
high schools, living in the same neighbourhood. He
was later to graduate and emigrate to America.

Another good friend was Ibrahim, a Palestinian,
who also lived in their neighbourhood. He was a
bright student and they had some good times
together. But Hasib wouldn't allow this friendship to
develop too far. Palestinians were different and you
didn't mix with them. Oh yes, you supported their
cause against the Israelis and even fought for them if
necessary, but you kept your distance. He had
refused several marriage proposals for his daughters,
that had come from well placed Palestinians. The
Damascus Sunni elite looked down on them as on so

many other groups. The old tribal loyalties and taboos were still very strong.

The university campus was in the heart of Damascus, just behind the exhibition centre. It had beautiful grounds and the buildings were very attractive in the old French colonial style. Later a new campus was built further out for the humanities and arts faculties.

Sometimes on his way home from university, Nabil would slip into a Christian Church out of curiosity to get to know their form of worship. One day, as he slipped furtively into the back rows of an orthodox church his father's chauffeur, Joseph, saw him. Nabil was frightened. What if Joseph told his father? It would get him into endless trouble. He couldn't sleep that night, and early next morning he phoned Joseph and begged him not to tell anyone about it. Joseph promised he wouldn't, and he kept his word.

'But why did you do it?' Joseph asked Nabil.

'Oh, I just wanted to see how Christians pray. It was merely curiosity,' he replied.

Nabil was a rather introverted young fellow. Something always seemed to keep him from sharing his real feelings and innermost thoughts with his family. His father was too strict and distant, his mother treated him as if he was still a little boy, Anwar was too snobbish and too involved in religion and in pressuring Nabil to join him in his devotions. Nabil shrank from the extremist environment Anwar moved in and it created a barrier between them. Only his middle sister, Amal, understood him. He

felt at ease with her and could tell her some of his
secrets, his romantic feelings for some girl or other,
his reflections on life. She always stood by him when
he had conflicts with Hasib.

Uncle Muhammad persuaded Hasib not to allow
his girls to study at university. They had all finished
high school and would dearly have liked to go on
into higher education. They pleaded and wept, they
got Fairouz on their side to support their claims, but
to no avail. University would have a bad influence on
them and expose them to the outside world as no
decent Muslim girl should be exposed. The only
thing for them to do was stay at home until they got
married — the earlier the better.

Jamileh was the first to get married, and her
husband was a young electrical engineer who was
very religious and ran a study group in the local
mosque — he had been one of Nabil's teachers there.

Amal, Nabil's favourite sister, got married to a
businessman from a good family who imported spare
parts for cars. Though a good Muslim, he was easy
going and tolerant, and would often support Nabil
and his lifestyle against the more stringent demands
of Hasib and Muhammad.

Iman was married last, to a diplomat working at
the presidential palace. From him Nabil heard a lot
about the inner workings of government, the in-
trigues and power struggles. He arranged for the
whole family to visit the palace one day and drink
coffee there. It was very impressive, and Hasib made
contacts with even more influential people through
his youngest son-in-law.

Jamileh's husband tried to get Nabil involved in religious activities. This brother-in-law used to preach the Friday sermons in various mosques that didn't have a qualified preacher. One Friday he invited Nabil to go with him to a village mosque some distance from Damascus and be the prayer leader and preacher. There was a small congregation of about twenty farmers. Nabil stood in front of them all leading the prayers, then went up to the pulpit and read out the sermon his brother-in-law had written out for him. It was the first and the last time. He begged not to have to do it again — it was embarrassing for him, he was too shy.

Another time this same brother-in-law took Nabil to a Sufi (mystical Muslim) meeting held in the house of a very famous Islamic leader, Sheikh Hasan Habbannaki. Nabil had never seen any thing like it before. They prayed and danced until they got into a trance-like state. Some couldn't control themselves any more. One man in the centre of the crowd was shouting out verses in a frenzy and weeping. Suddenly he fell down in a fit, his limbs jerking — the onlookers said God's spirit had now entered him and he was in a special state of grace.

Most of these religious leaders were in trouble with the authorities because of their activities and weren't allowed to leave Syria. When they wanted to go on the pilgrimage, they all came to Hasib who managed to arrange passports and permits for them and for their wives because of his position in the ministry of interior. It wasn't easy — he had to bend some rules to do it, but he felt it his duty to help the

spiritual leaders perform such an important religious
ceremony.

There was a lot of political activity in the
university at that time, many groups were vying for
influence and trying to recruit students to their ranks.
The main confrontation was between the Muslim
Brotherhood and the Ba'ath Party. Both groups
invited Nabil and his friends to join, but Nabil was
not interested. He was appalled at the violence used
by the Brotherhood to attain their political goals.
Many prominent people were assassinated, including
a well liked lecturer, a PhD, who was shot dead in
his office by a student as he was preparing for a
lecture, the only reason for the assassination being
that he was an 'Alawi. Most students were upset, but
there was little they could do about it.

Some students joined the Ba'ath party group, and
they were later rewarded by being advanced very
quickly to high positions in the government.

Nabil worked hard at his studies. There were lots
of seminars to attend, papers to hand in, exams to
pass. It was a very busy time for him. Two hours a
week were dedicated to military training – a new
system recently introduced by the authorities. It was
compulsory, and it meant that later six months
would be deducted from your national service term.
Nabil and some of his friends, still immature and
spoilt youngsters, didn't take it too seriously, and
were in constant trouble with the officers in charge
of the course. In the summer holidays they had to
participate in a twenty day basic training course at a
military camp, living in tents, wearing uniforms and

drilling. Nabil rebelled: he refused to eat the army rations, didn't get up on time and disobeyed orders. The officer was furious and sentenced him to isolated imprisonment for some days in a tent out on its own under armed guard. They were going to shave off all his hair too.

Hasib and Fairouz came to visit the camp at just the right moment. Fairouz was always very concerned for her little boy in the harsh army surroundings. She had prepared lots of his favourite home-made food and persuaded Hasib to drive her to the camp. Nabil was brought to the visitors' tent and told them what had happened. Fairouz was shocked. Hasib wanted to leave him to reap what he had sown – it would be a good lesson for him.

'Oh no', wailed Fairouz, 'we can't let them do this to him. You must speak to the officer.'

Hasib finally gave in and spoke to the commanding officer. It was agreed that he would free Nabil on condition that he promised to obey orders and show exemplary behaviour till the end of the course. Nabil, who was already planning to escape from this miserable situation (the penalty for which would have been no pass to the next study year), readily agreed and rejoined the other soldiers. What a relief!

In the long summer holidays, both Anwar and Nabil worked for an uncle of theirs who had an agency for German office machines. It was good work experience, they earned some money, and, most important of all, it kept them off the streets and out of trouble. Hasib insisted they must take up these jobs and not be idle.

Nabil enjoyed student life in the company of a select group of special friends. There were some twenty of them, boys and girls from good Sunni families, who formed their own exclusive clique. They all did well in their studies and as a result were well liked by the lecturers. Their main aim was to enjoy the university years together. Religion and politics were taboo for them, they preferred the cinema, discos and parties. They organised a trip together to the beaches of Latakia on the Mediterranean and had picnics in the Ghuta oasis around Damascus.

Two of the girls, Rena and Iman, had their eyes on Nabil. Both of them would have liked to see him ask their parents for their hand in marriage. But Nabil wouldn't even think about it at that stage. He enjoyed the carefree bachelor life and felt he was much too young to contemplate marriage. Girls in Syrian society were under tremendous pressure to marry young and get settled as soon as possible. He felt sorry for them, he enjoyed their company, but he wasn't in love with any of them and didn't want to get tied down yet.

Hasib and Fairouz were also very interested in getting their sons married to the right girls as soon as possible. It was still the custom for parents to arrange the marriages of their children. Fairouz spent over a year looking for the right girl for Anwar, checking out families and backgrounds. She wanted the perfect match – a good-looking, well-educated girl from a religious and wealthy Sunni background, with a good reputation and a family you could get on with as relations. The women of the family would spend many hours discussing different girls, describing them in detail, comparing their virtues. There was a lot of discussion going on in the family about this – everyone was involved.

Finally Fairouz found the perfect match. After this, the Muslim custom was to repeat a special prayer twice just before you went to sleep, asking God for guidance. Any dreams you had that night were assumed to be God's answer to your petition. If they were pleasant, the answer was 'yes'. If you had nightmares, it was obviously 'no'.

Grandmother, Father, Mother, uncles and aunts all performed this ritual that same night. Next morning they all reported pleasant dreams – one had dreamt she was swimming in beautifully clear water, the other that he was walking high up in the mountains with a wonderful view all around him, the grass green, the sun shining – it was all positive, so they took it to be God's confirmation of their plans and the marriage arrangements were made. They were married just after Anwar graduated from university. In fact, they had considerable marital trouble during their first year, they had not known each other at all before their wedding, and the family had often to mediate and arbitrate until they got used to life together.

Once Anwar, the eldest son, was settled, the pressure was turned on to Nabil: 'Choose a girl. Get married. Give your parents the pleasure of seeing you settle down. Tell us if there is any particular girl you fancy.'

Their real choice for him was a cousin, five years younger than himself, the daughter of Hasib's youngest brother. She was very pretty, had studied pharmacology, and her father had set up a pharmacy specifically for her. He also bought her a house and a car, so that she was a very attractive proposition for any suitor. She and her mother would visit Fairouz almost every day. Hasib was greatly in favour of the match: marrying a cousin was in line with Muslim culture. It strengthened family ties and kept the wealth in the family. Fairouz was very insistent too; she would nag Nabil about it every day:

'Nabil, this is the right girl for you. Just say "yes". You don't have to marry right now, but let us settle the arrangements.'

Nabil wouldn't agree. He liked the girl, but she was more like a sister with whom he had played as a child. He couldn't imagine her as his wife — and he did not want to be bound by marital ties. He wanted to remain free for as long as possible. This caused many arguments and discussions — but he wouldn't give in.

Anwar got deeply involved with the Muslim Brotherhood during his university years, although no one in the family knew it at that time. He continued to shine academically, and on graduation was offered a teaching position at university which he accepted. He even wrote a textbook on civil engineering which is still being used. Nabil helped with the typesetting, and Hasib, the proud father, paid to have it published. It sold well and got Anwar started early on his business career.

His final project was to design the foundations for the largest office building in Damascus. Nabil took a special course in technical drawing so he could help in preparing the blueprints. It was a great success.

The confrontation between the government and the Muslim Brotherhood flared up again in 1980. Many of the Brotherhood were arrested, including Anwar's best friend (of whom nothing more was ever heard). Hasib was very worried when he realised that his eldest son was involved in the Brotherhood. He knew that Anwar was in very grave danger. A family council was called and it was decided to get him out of the country as soon as possible. Fairouz recited the whole Qur'an in two days as penance for his ransom.

Using his position and connections Hasib managed to get the Minister of Interior to grant a special permit for Anwar to leave Syria. He first had to pay $5000 to the military authorities to have him freed from army service, then he obtained a passport for him and put him on a plane to the United Arab Emirates. He was in such a hurry that he didn't have time to get him an entry visa to the UAE, but he arranged for a friend to meet Anwar at Dubai Airport and help him to obtain a transit visa for seven days which was later extended. Anwar eventually settled in the UAE and started his own civil engineering and construction business there. He did quite well for himself, and his wife followed him some months later flying out to Dubai accompanied by Fairouz.

Hasib was relieved when Anwar was safely out of

Syria. Because of his position in the ministry of interior he knew that the confrontation between the government and the Muslim Brotherhood was bound to intensify. It was a 'no holds barred' struggle for power in the Syrian state and neither side would compromise. His fears were fully justified when in 1982 the brotherhood organised the uprising in the town of Hama. It was finally brutally suppressed by the security forces using heavy artillery and tanks to destroy large parts of this old city, and it is reckoned that more than 20,000 people were killed in that confrontation. Thousands of the brotherhood members and sympathisers all over Syria simply disappeared and were never heard of again.

Hasib had originally wanted both his boys to serve in the Syrian army, but Fairouz protested. She did not want her dear boys endangered by any involvement in the fighting in Lebanon, where the Syrian army occasionally fought the various Muslim groups as well as the Christians in an effort to ensure Syrian hegemony over the divided land. She was also afraid of a possible war against the arch-enemy Israel evolving out of the Lebanese débacle. Neither of them believed that the Syrian army could win in an all-out confrontation with Israel.

With both the government and the army controlled by the 'Alawis, the Sunni families did not feel morally obliged to send their sons to the army if they could avoid doing so. The 'Alawis were felt to be almost as much enemies of true Islam as the Israelis – they were only consolidating their own power under the guise of a Holy War against Israel, so why fight for them? One rule of Islam is that you first fight the enemy nearest to you before attacking those further away. Sunni religious leaders actually issued Fatwas in the early eighties claiming that killing an 'Alawi was as meritorious an act as killing an Israeli.

As far as they were concerned, the other communities could do the fighting – the Sunni élite would do the ruling! Only the rich, however, could avoid conscription, by paying the high sum of $5000 as ransom for each son and then sending them abroad for five years. After that period they could legally return to Syria without having to serve.

Having made this arrangement for Anwar under the pressure of events, Hasib and Fairouz decided to do the same for Nabil. On his graduation from the university in 1982, they paid the $5000 fine and put him on a plane to the UAE – this time with the necessary entry visa. Anwar waited for him at the airport and took him under his wing, giving him a position in his own company.

7

In the Arabian Gulf

The town of Dubai is the capital of the oil-rich
emirate of Dubai, one of the seven that constitute the
United Arab Emirates of the Arabian Gulf. In the
1980s it was experiencing a boom due to the influx
of oil revenues and it attracted people from all over
the Arab world looking for well paid employment. It
had a population of some 275,000 people at the
time, and had recently been thoroughly modernised.
It was actually the largest city of the federation, its
economic centre, and was connected by road to Abu-
Dhabi and Ras al-Khaymah, the other two important
towns in the area.

By the time of Nabil's arrival in Dubai, Anwar had
become well settled and successful in his business
venture. Nabil worked in Anwar's company in
Dubai for the first six months. He did some
accounting for his brother and was a jack of all
trades, doing whatever jobs were necessary. This
wasn't too fulfilling or exciting.

After the first few weeks of living with Anwar, he

rented a flat for himself, so that he could have some privacy. He found working for his own brother difficult, mixing family relationship with business, and he tried to get another job as soon as possible. A friend of Anwar's who ran a trading company needed an accountant, so Nabil was happy to accept that position and worked there for seven months.

He noticed that this company was going downhill, so he decided to change jobs again. Anwar was helpful in introducing him to another friend of his, a Syrian named Ahmad, who had established a large and flourishing Islamic publishing house with branches in all Arabic states and in many other countries. They published new editions of the Qur'an, Hadith, religious commentaries and reference books which were highly popular all over the Muslim world. Nabil was taken on as general manager of the firm's branch in Dubai. He was quite successful, establishing its basic accounting procedures and expanding its clientele and sales volume.

Life in Dubai settled into a routine. The pay was very good, he had a pleasant flat, and in order to enjoy his leisure time better he became a member of the exclusive Hyatt-Regency Hotel Club with its swimming pool and sporting facilities. Daily he would go there with some of his friends to swim, take a sauna, play tennis, exercise, or play a game of chess, which was becoming his main hobby at that time.

Ahmad his boss, the company owner, became very fond of him and would often ask Nabil to accompany him for lunch or dinner in some high class restaurant. Life was good and the future seemed even more promising. Occasionally he would be sent abroad on company business to Kuwait, Lebanon, Saudi Arabia, even to Spain, Germany, France and Britain. It was exciting and gave him a feeling of importance.

Once a year he had to take his passport to the Syrian embassy to have it stamped, so that he could return to Syria once the five years were over. Hasib and Fairouz would visit their sons twice a year, happy to see them doing so well for themselves. They knew Anwar couldn't ever return to Syria but looked forward to Nabil's return at the end of the five year absence.

Nabil made some friends, mainly Syrians living in the oil-rich gulf to make money. The Syrians were part of the large number of expatriate Arabs and other foreigners working in the UAE. They were never given citizenship, as the locals were afraid they would take over. But the Syrians were one of the most respected groups of foreigners. Together with the Lebanese they were valued for their education and trusted by the nationals. They were seen as businesslike and honest. The Jordanians were too much like the local Beduin stock to be accepted. They didn't like taking orders from others, preferring to be the bosses who ordered others around. The Egyptians were seen as weak and submissive, a legacy of their history under the Pharaohs! The Palestinians were hated, although everyone was ready to fight for their cause. They were viewed as trouble-makers and politically dangerous.

The local UAE people were mainly of Beduin descent, first generation city dwellers. Nabil and his like were too westernised for their taste, not Arabic or Islamic enough. They had strict rules about allowing other Arabs to work in their country. Anwar had to give a 51% share in his company to a UAE citizen whose sole contribution was that of giving his name as co-owner. He did no work, took no risk, but pocketed $50,000 a year for his services! All he ever did was to fingerprint the contract when it came up for renewal each year (he couldn't read or write).

At the bottom of UAE society were the immigrant workers from Pakistan, India and Bangladesh. They did all the dirty, menial work no one else wanted to do. Although they were Muslims, they were treated scornfully as mere servants. They washed the cars, took the clothes to the laundry, cleaned the flats and offices and swept the streets. Nabil found them very useful – he would pay a fellow to start the car up for him in the hot sun so that the air conditioning could begin to work, and after a few minutes he would be able to get into the cool car straight from his flat or office. They brought tea or coffee to his desk at work or to the business meetings he attended. They would do anything for their pay.

They were paid for their services, but it was a paltry sum and they were treated like dirt. Anwar would think nothing of slapping one of them in the face in front of everyone else if the man hadn't done the job to his satisfaction.

When setting up book exhibitions for his new company, Nabil would employ some of them to do all the manual work, setting up the shelves and displays, cleaning up the place, whilst he and the other employees sat around drinking coffee and chatting until everything was ready. No one ever thanked them for their hard work.

Actually, Nabil discovered that they were good, honest and humble people. They never complained, they were hard-working and loyal. They never argued or talked back like the Beduin or other population groups. They would call their bosses, including Nabil, 'Arbab', meaning 'Lords': 'Yes, Arbab, okay Arbab, as you say, Arbab'. It made their employers feel rather proud, but the truth was that these people from the Indian subcontinent actually preferred working for Syrians and other foreigners than for the local Arabs who treated them even worse.

Nabil had two special friends. Amir was an agronomist and a free thinker. Mu'in he knew from the mosque study group in Damascus. Both had left Syria, like himself, in order to evade army service. Each one tried to influence Nabil in his own way and pull him towards his preferred lifestyle. Whilst Amir took him out to enjoy the pleasures of this life offered in Dubai, Mu'in would try to get him to accompany him to the mosque and to prayers. He had established a study group in a local Dubai mosque, and Nabil sometimes went with him out of habit – he was used to Islamic studies, it was part of his background. In Dubai and all of the Gulf region, Islam is a very strong social force, and everyone is expected to attend regularly at prayer times. You get a good name if you are perceived to be an observant and pious Muslim, and this attracts business!

Nabil used much of his free time to read books. He was in the publishing business now where books were easily accessible to him, and he established a very good library for himself in his flat. He read a lot about Islam, but also general reference works and science books. He was thinking a lot, searching for answers to the questions he had always had about the meaning of life.

Living on his own in Dubai, Nabil felt his personality developing and maturing. For the first time in his life he was truly independent. He was completely on his own – no parents to report to or to fuss over him. There was no one to dictate to him who should be his friends or what he should do with his leisure time. He thoroughly enjoyed this new freedom.

He concentrated all his energies into developing his career. He improved business procedures in the firm and increased the sales volume. He contacted new clients and pushed for more orders. It was gratifying to see the Dubai branch for which he was responsible flourish, and his boss was pleased with his accomplishments.

Yet deep down in his heart there was a feeling of unease, a disturbing vacuum. He still had many questions about religion and about life for which he could find no answers. There was no one he could talk to about these subjects in the environment in which he found himself. People there just didn't ask such questions and didn't seem to be bothered by any doubts or qualms. They seemed satisfied with the old formulas given by traditional Islam, and feeling confident in their religion would concentrate on improving their material situation in the feverish economic activity of the Gulf. They seemed oblivious to the many contradictions that stared Nabil in the face day after day.

8

The Discovery

Although Nabil had everything he needed materially, he often felt an emptiness inside. Something was missing in his life. He often analysed himself and tried to find the cause. What was wrong with him? What was the problem? After all, he firmly believed in God, he was moderately religious, attended the mosque, studied Islam. But God somehow seemed very remote and impersonal, an unknown force somewhere out there, beyond his grasp and comprehension. What did God actually mean for him personally? Was there a way to discover such a meaning?

He remembered Hasib talking to Fairouz about his religious life. He would say: 'Look, Fairouz, I have done everything a good Muslim ought to do. I pray five times each day, I have been seven times on the Haj, I give the prescribed Zakat alms to the poor, I do all that God has commanded men to do – I do

hope that God will accept me.' He had a shaky hope
that his deeds would merit him a place in Paradise –
but he had no assurance. Nabil couldn't understand
this, it was one of the questions that often bothered
him: if Hasib had done everything required of him,
why was there no guarantee of Paradise? Why did he
still have to fear the possibility of ending in hell?

The Islamic teaching was that only God knows
what will happen to you in eternity. He alone has the
final decision, and man has no assurance whatsoever
concerning his fate. This seemed to imply that God
could be arbitrary, and that no matter how hard you
tried to win his favour, he could at the last moment
decide to cast you into hell. His will was supreme
and there was no questioning his decrees, even if they
seemed capricious to us. There were many traditional stories to illustrate this, stories about evil
people who God decided to send to Paradise, and
about good people who he sent to hell. It didn't seem
fair or logical. What kind of God was this?

Nabil realised that to Hasib and other devout
Muslims, God seemed like a hard taskmaster, just
waiting for them to slip and commit a mistake or a
sin so that he could pounce on them in judgement.
They actually lived in fear of ending up in hell, and
worried about it a lot. Hasib used also to say to
Fairouz: 'If I die, please don't forget to recite the
Qur'an for me three or four times a year, and make
sure you regularly visit the cemetery with my friends
to pray for me.' These rituals were supposed to lift
the soul of the deceased up to a better place in the
afterlife; but could they really trust their families and

friends to perform them faithfully, year after year, after their departure? The chances seemed pretty slim. It was all rather depressing.

Nabil would daily pick up the mail at the firm's post box in the central post office in Dubai. One day he found a leaflet in Arabic sent to the firm's address from somewhere in Lebanon. It was about the Prophet Issa (Jesus) and pointed out that he was actually a manifestation of God and the only way to happiness. Nabil read it, then threw it away thinking, 'How stupid can you get!' From then on, every couple of months, a new leaflet or booklet would arrive — sometimes mailed in Germany, sometimes in Lebanon and sometimes in Cyprus. He realised that it was illegal and could have reported it to the authorities — but something kept him back. He read all these papers — about how Issa was the Messiah who had died for the sins of mankind, how he loved all men and offered them free salvation. Nabil wasn't convinced by what he read. It was diametrically opposed to his strongly held Muslim beliefs. Yes, Issa was a great Prophet, but he was a man like all the other prophets. God can have no son, and it is a grave sin to associate a man with him. Issa didn't die — God caused someone else to die in his place and took him up to heaven. Nabil knew all the traditional Muslim arguments against Christianity, and he threw the leaflets away in disgust.

One of the leaflets offered more information and a free Bible if you wrote to an address in Cyprus. Nabil filled in the attached coupon and sent it off. He did want to know more. In spite of his prejudice, he could glimpse some new ideas that aroused his curiosity.

Some time later he received the Bible, a small magazine called 'The Key' and some more leaflets. He kept them in his flat, and in the evenings would sit and read them. The Bible was in modern, easy Arabic – compared to the Qur'an it seemed rather flat and unexciting. No rhythm, no music, no lilt. It sounded like a normal secular book. Still, something pushed him to read on, although there was a lot he didn't understand.

Around that time Nabil made the acquaintance of an American businessman in Dubai. Henry Amherst represented several western publishers and sold scientific books to schools, universities and government offices. He used Nabil's book exhibitions as an outlet for his books and was a very good customer. Nabil could also sell him some of their own publications and slowly got to know him better. He liked this friendly, frank American who was scrupulously honest in all his business deals. Eventually, they became close friends. They would often go out to have lunch together, or to the beach for a swim. Then they would sip some coffee and chat. They had lots of fun together and enjoyed each other's company.

Ahmad, Nabil's boss, wasn't happy with this new friend. He didn't like Westerners, especially not Americans, and he urged Nabil to limit his contacts with Henry to business matters only. This caused some friction, as Nabil resented this interference in his private affairs.

Henry was married, but his wife and children lived in the States. He would spend the cooler months of the year in Dubai, then take a long summer break of four months to be with his family in the USA.

Nabil really liked Henry. He admired his honesty, the way he was always ready to help, his kind and thoughtful manner. These were traits Nabil hadn't noticed in his other friends. What was his secret?

Henry did his best to help Nabil in his job. He had been working in Dubai for many years, and had many valuable contacts with key business and government people. He introduced Nabil to some of them and suggested others who might be interested in the Islamic books. At that time the firm had just come out with a very expensive edition of the Qur'an – leather binding, gold lettering – it was beautiful, and Henry's contacts helped Nabil to sell many copies of it.

As they got to know each other better, Nabil one day mentioned casually that he had received a Bible and some Christian material through the post. Henry didn't respond at the time, but later that week asked Nabil if he was really reading the Injil. Nabil told him that he was, and that there was a lot in it that he didn't understand. Henry talked to him for a while about his own personal faith as a Christian, how he sincerely believed that Issa was divine and had died for his sins. He didn't press the subject any further, but from that time onwards, they often spoke about religion. Usually it was Nabil who would first broach the subject.

In typical Middle Eastern manner, Nabil often violently disagreed with what Henry said about Issa. But Henry always remained cool and presented his beliefs in a logical manner. This impressed Nabil who had expected a shouting match. He was pleased that they could talk to each other about their respective religions without getting upset, and still remain good friends.

One day Henry asked Nabil if he would like to visit him at his home where a few friends would be gathered for prayer. Nabil thought: 'There's nothing wrong with prayer,' and agreed. He went over to Henry's flat and met some of Henry's friends gathered in the living room. They were all Westerners. They drank coffee and chatted for a while, then Henry asked for people to share prayer requests and they started praying to God about them.

Nabil listened carefully. When they opened with 'Heavenly Father' he added 'Ya Rab' ('Oh Lord') under his breath. When they closed in Jesus' name – he could see nothing wrong with it. After all Issa (Jesus) was a great Prophet and God was sure to answer prayers in a Holy Man's name. What really struck Nabil was how informal and personal it all was. They didn't recite formal prayers from a prayer book. They spoke to God as to a personal caring father, asking him to grant personal requests and needs. God seemed very near to them – not far off and unreachable as in Islam. It was a new experience which gave Nabil much food for thought.

Something inside him said: 'No Nabil, this is wrong, it is not for you, it is not Muslim.' But then all they did seemed perfectly right, and he was attracted to them.

This was a confusing time for Nabil. He attended more of these 'get-togethers', read the Bible and thought about the issues involved. There was so much he didn't understand, but Henry encouraged him to keep reading and praying for guidance.

Reading through the Injil of Matta, some sayings of Issa stood out and challenged him in a special way by their moral force: 'But I tell you: Love your enemies and pray for those who persecute you, that you may be sons of your Father in heaven' (Matt.5;44,45), was one of them. It was shocking! It was so opposed to all he had been taught in his Muslim background. It caused a long and heated discussion with Henry.

'Look, Henry,' said Nabil, 'no one ever told me to love my enemies. We are taught to hate them and actively fight them. After all, that's what enemies are for. This is an impossible demand. I'll never be able to love an Israeli — they are enemies we are supposed to fight.'

'You're quite right Nabil,' answered Henry, 'it is very difficult, in fact it is impossible. Many things Issa asks us to do are beyond natural man's power to perform. This is exactly why we need him and his power in our lives. This is why you need to believe in him.'

'Believing in him is easy,' said Nabil, 'we Muslims believe in him as a great prophet, we believe he was born of the virgin Maryam of God's spirit. But how can I accept him as God? God is one, unique, different, invisible, beyond human reach. I can never accept him as the son of God. That goes against all my upbringing and teaching.'.

Another verse that struck him was the one where Issa says: 'It is not the healthy that need a doctor but the sick . . . For I have not come to call the righteous but sinners' (Matt.9;12,13). It really amazed him when he first read these words.

'Did Issa mean just the bodily sick?' he asked Henry. 'Was he not interested in normal, healthy people?'

'Jesus means all of us,' explained Henry. 'We are all sick with sin. If you think that because you keep a few religious rules you are not a sinner, you are mistaken.'

Nabil was very touched by these revelations. Although he considered himself an honest man and a good Muslim, he was never really happy or relaxed, never at peace with himself. He was a loner, reading, thinking, avoiding society as much as possible, not liking to mix with other people. He had always been a worrier and his religion hadn't helped him so far in solving these personal problems. When he read the words of Issa he felt something stirring within his soul, a hint of peace and fulfillment he had never felt before.

Nabil realised that to Henry and his friends God was near and personal, a loving father whom they could trust, and to whom they could bring personal requests for the mundane things of life. This was a revelation. Prayer had always been a ritual to be performed in the prescribed manner without asking why. God required it, and that was enough reason to perform it. If you didn't you could expect a horrible punishment. He had never experienced prayer for personal needs, or for the needs of others, but for Henry and his friends this seemed to be the most natural thing on earth.

They spoke about having a personal relationship with a God who loved you and who accepted you as you were, a God who had forgiven all your sins because Issa had borne the punishment for them when he died on the cross. It was unbelievable – but very attractive! Imagine not having to strain yourself to earn merit with God, to be able to relax and not worry whether you had kept all the requirements for that day, to have the assurance that your place in heaven is guaranteed – it all seemed too good to be true.

Every night, before he fell asleep, Nabil would first recite the Shahada thirty-three times with the help of a rosary. It was a deeply inculcated habit he had been taught by his mother as a little child. Should he die in his sleep, he was then sure to die as a Muslim, not a Kaffir. No matter what sins he had committed during the day, this prayer made sure he was a good Muslim for that night. Throughout these difficult months Nabil continued this habit, comforted by the knowledge that he was still a good Muslim.

Finally the time came for Henry's long summer holiday. Before leaving he asked Nabil to keep an eye on his business and occasionally check his account books. Nabil was touched by this display of trust. Henry also invited him to visit him in the USA, but

Nabil wasn't planning any trip so far away. He accompanied Henry to the airport, and on the way Henry advised him to go on reading the Injil even if he didn't understand it all.

'Just take it literally,' he said. 'Don't try reading between the lines.' He knew that in Islam you must try reading the Qur'an between the lines, you must search for the hidden meaning behind the words.

He left and there was a gap in Nabil's life. He really missed his friend. He didn't know what to do with himself in his free time, he had become so used to spending time with Henry.

Several months later Nabil was due for a long holiday. In a sudden moment of inspiration he decided to spend it in the USA! He would visit a very good Syrian friend of his, Kamal, who was now studying in Boston, and he might be able to visit Henry too. It was much easier for a Syrian to get an American visa in the UAE than it was in Syria itself. The company would pay half of his expenses – so he decided to go ahead with this plan.

Nabil flew from Dubai to JFK airport in New York and took a bus to Boston, where Kamal picked him up and took him to his flat. He stayed with Kamal and enjoyed being with his friend after all these years of separation. He also tried contacting Henry to arrange a visit, but Henry was away from home on business and the visit couldn't be fitted in.

One day, a Lebanese Christian friend of Kamal, Joseph, came for a visit. Kamal introduced him to Nabil and they sat and chatted. Joseph told him about his previous work in Beirut – he had been involved in visiting prisoners in the Beiruti jails and telling them about Jesus. Nabil was astonished.

'These people got what they deserved for their crimes,' said Nabil. 'God arranged for them to get into jail, it is his will, they deserve their punishment, so why bother with them any more?'

'Oh no,' said Joseph. 'God still loves them and wants to save them. He has something more for them.'

'God definitely has nothing more for them,' answered Nabil, 'he is punishing them for their sins.'

Joseph spoke rather disrespectfully about Muhammad and that infuriated Nabil, who almost lost control of himself and would have hit him. Joseph insinuated that Muhammad was an insignificant man and came from an unrespectable family.

'Hold on,' shouted Nabil, 'you must be crazy. Every one knows he came from the Quraish and they were the noblest family in Mecca. No Muslim will ever listen to your message if you distort the facts in this way.'

Some days later another Lebanese man visited with his son and with them came an American friend named Steve Mailer. As was customary in Arabic culture, they all sipped coffee and chatted. Nabil was impressed by Steve. He reminded him very much of his friend Henry. He had worked for many years in a Muslim country and knew the social patterns and culture. He spoke like Henry and Nabil was almost sure that he shared a similar belief. When he left, they arranged for Nabil to visit him the next day in his home in New Jersey.

Kamal dropped Nabil off at Steve's place and they had a long conversation about religion. Nabil explained his situation, his spiritual search, the fact that he just couldn't go on living like this, torn between two faiths. He loved his family, background and society, but he had come to believe that Issa the Messiah was the only way to God.

Steve explained that Issa was God come in the flesh who had offered himself as a perfect sacrifice for us undeserving sinners. Religious duties couldn't save us from being judged by a holy God. We needed a mediator who would reconcile us to God and this mediator was Issa, who by his death had obtained divine forgiveness for all who believed in him.

'Steve', said Nabil, 'I really believe all you say, I want to become a true follower of Issa.'

'Not so fast, young man,' answered Steve, 'let's first pray about it and see how God will guide.'

They prayed together and Nabil left and returned to Kamal's home. Some days later he was on the plane flying back to Dubai having spent forty-five days in the USA.

Sitting on the plane he was still confused, lost in thought, weeping inwardly and praying to God for guidance. 'I can't go on like this' he said to God, 'I can't go on living a lie. I can't go with Anwar to the mosque or talk to mother as if I was still a good Muslim, as if nothing had changed. I can't be a Muslim during the day and pray to Issa at night — show me what to do.'

Back in Dubai he got into his old routine of work and leisure, but he had no peace. One night he just couldn't fall asleep. He went out for a walk, knowing that he must face up to his situation. He couldn't continue living two separate lives at one and the same time. Walking the dark streets he finally came to a clear cut decision. He believed in Issa, he believed that Issa had died for his sins, so he would become a true follower of the Messiah.

It was a momentous decision that would totally change his life, though at that time he didn't foresee all the difficulties ahead of him. Having finally come to a firm decision he felt happier than ever before. This was the happiest moment of his whole life. He felt at peace with himself and with God. He had made the right choice!

He went back to his flat, and before sleeping recited the 'Shahada' as usual. It was an old habit and died hard. The devil whispered: 'If you don't do it and then don't wake up in the morning, you will have died a Kaffir.' It was a few months before he could stop this evening ritual.

When Henry arrived back in Dubai, Nabil happily shared his decision with his friend. Henry wasn't altogether convinced about it. He felt Nabil was in too much of a hurry. Basically he was worried for his friend, knowing better than Nabil the grave consequences of such a step for a Muslim in his own society.

'You have made a mistake,' he told Nabil, 'you can remain a Muslim and worship Issa at the same time. God will understand. If people find out about your decision it will be very tough for you.'

Nabil wasn't convinced. In Islam you have to

mention Muhammad and bless him and pray for him hundreds of times. You approach God on your own merits, not through a mediator who did it all for you, or through a sacrifice. You deny that God can have a son. No, he couldn't go on in that way.

Henry however proved to be a great support to him in spite of this disagreement. He spent much time with him, praying, reading and explaining the Injil, helping him to understand what it meant to be a true follower of Issa. Nabil enjoyed those times.

However, when they moved from the Injil to the Old Testament, the Tawrah, Nabil received a shock – it was all about Israel, the arch-enemy of the Arabs! How could God have given them so many promises and privileges? Of course in Islam it is recognised that God revealed the Tawrah and the Zabur to the Jews, and that Moses and other great prophets rose amongst them. But they had disobeyed God and corrupted the scriptures, which was why God was angry with them and had punished them, and he then sent his last messenger to men, Muhammad, with the final and true scriptures, the Qur'an.

It was difficult for Nabil to accept that the Old Testament had the true story of God's dealings with man in the past, and that the Qur'an's version was garbled. The whole tenor was too political, too relevant to the modern day Palestinian problem and all the emotions it arouses in Muslim Arabs to be easily acceptable. It took time, but God slowly changed his thinking until he accepted that the whole Bible, from Genesis through to Revelation, was God's Holy Book.

Nabil noticed that his character was changing, or rather being changed, since he first believed in Issa. He had an inner desire to spend time in prayer and in Bible reading. This wasn't the compulsion of duty he had felt in Islam, but rather a joyful attraction. He didn't have to look at his watch to see if it was time for prayers, it was his heart's desire to pray and he spent much time in talking to God. He didn't have to – he wanted to! He was really happy; for the first time in his life the emptiness was gone.

He was still living in an Islamic world, working as manager of an Islamic publisher. No one knew of his decision. He read and prayed in the evenings in the privacy of his own flat. Outwardly nothing had changed; he didn't speak about his decision to anyone and kept it completely private and confidential – but Anwar and his boss noticed a change. They noticed that he neglected the mosque. Ahmad once visited his flat and saw an Injil lying there on the table. He was very upset.

Things came to a head between him and Anwar and Ahmad. They had a terrible quarrel and Nabil was fired unjustly with no pay and no compensation. He decided to leave Dubai and fly to Poland.

It was as well that he had acted so quickly in contacting the Syrian consul and getting his military problem sorted out, because soon after their quarrel Anwar phoned their parents in Damascus and told them about the change he had noticed in Nabil. They were very worried, and Fairouz phoned him a few times to reassure herself that he was still a Muslim.

'Recite the Shahada for me,' she asked him, 'I

want to hear you saying it with my own ears.' He did it, not wanting to hurt her feelings. She would have died on the spot had he refused.

'I heard you have become a Christian,' she continued. 'Is it true? Why do you have a Bible in your house, isn't the Qur'an good enough? If I ever hear that you have become a Christian, you will not be my son any more, I will harden my heart towards you.'

This was a serious threat for a devout Muslim, because without your mother's and father's blessing you have no hope of paradise.

She was somewhat reassured by hearing the Shahada from his own lips, but Hasib and Anwar certainly weren't. Hasib wouldn't get in touch with Nabil personally – he used Anwar as a go-between to express his disapproval and shock. Nabil was hurt by his father's hardness. He felt a great sense of relief as he boarded the plane and flew off to Europe away from it all.

9

Romance in Poland

Why did Nabil fly out to Warsaw? What drew him
to a communist country in eastern Europe?

During his work for Islamic Publishers Nabil had
flown to various countries to help coordinate the
special luxury edition of the Qur'an which they were
printing in Singapore. It was a large project, and
there were many meetings held to check for errors,
improve the layout, etc. It called for very meticulous
work, for even one error in a Qur'an would mean it
would have to be destroyed. It had to be perfect
down to the smallest vowel mark.

As his boss, Ahmad, didn't speak any English, he
delegated the job of dealing with those involved in
the non-Arabic speaking countries to Nabil, who
then travelled to Lebanon, Spain, France, Germany
and India to deal with the many aspects of this
prestigious project.

On one of these trips to Europe he was flying with

a colleague and they touched down in Warsaw for a transit to another flight. They had to wait several days, and the friend suggested that instead of waiting near the airport they take the train to Cracow and visit his cousin who was studying there. Not having anything better to do, Nabil agreed and off they went. The cousin invited them to join him at a party he was attending that same evening. At that party Nabil was introduced to a young Polish woman named Renata. She was a striking girl, tall and dark-haired with lustrous black eyes. Nabil was lovestruck from the first sight and for the first time in his life. He had resisted the idea of marriage for many years in spite of constant pressure from his mother. Every time she visited him in Dubai she would bring him news of various girls who were interested in him and try to persuade him to marry one of them. But he had consistently resisted all such pressures.

Meeting Renata changed all that. Suddenly all his defences were down and he could think only of her. She seemed to reciprocate his feelings: after all he was a good-looking mysterious stranger from the fabulously rich Arabian Gulf. They talked about themselves and their jobs. (Renata was working as a secretary for the town council and was very good at her job.) Nabil then invited her out to dinner the next day.

They had a romantic dinner out together and later Renata showed him the sights of her city. In true Arab fashion he proposed marriage there and then. Renata was somewhat taken aback – things were moving too fast! She thought she loved him, but needed time to think things over. So they agreed to a trial engagement for the time being which would bind them to each other in some measure, but at the same time leave a door open for reflection about the future and time to get to know each other better. Renata introduced Nabil to her mother and to her colleagues at work — they all liked him. They exchanged addresses and on his return to Dubai they kept up a lively correspondence enhanced by frequent phone calls.

From that time on Nabil would spend his holidays in Poland courting Renata. Soon they arrived at the final decision to get married, and started the official procedures for the necessary permits.

It was a crazy situation. They were both inexpressibly naïve about real life. They knew nothing about each other's background and culture, nothing about the political and legal maze they were entering into. They were certain that love would sort everything out.

Renata came from a very traditional and devout Roman Catholic family. It was a large family, and they were all very close to each other, spending much time together in each other's homes, talking a lot about anything and everything. Although they all said Nabil was a good man, and everyone seemed to like him, there was a general Polish mistrust of foreigners. 'He's a Muslim,' they would say to Renata, 'he may have other wives out there in the Gulf. He can divorce you any time he wishes. Take care!'

Strangely they had great difficulties in communicating. Renata spoke only a little English, having learnt some at school but had never had any practice, and she certainly knew no Arabic! At first they had to enlist the help of friends who acted as interpreters, and they also used a lot of sign language! Nabil, however, decided to learn Polish and threw himself into it with such determination that he could soon communicate to some extent. Renata at the same time started to improve her English — but it was a slow process.

Nabil tried to explain something about his new faith in Jesus to Renata, although the communication problem made it difficult. Although she was happy to hear that he, a Muslim, believed in Jesus, she was sure he must have fallen in with some dangerous sect such as the Jehovah Witnesses who were taboo to any sincere Catholic. For her and her family the Roman Catholic Church was the only true Christian Church, the only repository of the true faith and of salvation.

How could he, a Muslim, know anything about it? They tried explaining some of its doctrines to him, but to no avail. It was confusing for Nabil to face up to the different divisions in Christianity, but he kept to Henry's and Steve's advice to stick to the Bible as the ultimate authority for his faith, and he could see that some of the Catholic rites were far removed from it. He kept in touch with these two friends by phone and by letter and they advised him not to push his faith on Renata, but to let time do its part.

Nabil had tried to keep his relationship with Renata a secret from his family. However, a short while after he had first met her, a Syrian friend of his who had been living in Dubai and knew all about it returned to Syria and visited Hasib and Fairouz. He told them all he knew about Nabil's romance as well as about his interest in the Christian religion. It made them rather upset – not because they objected to his marrying a Christian woman which was allowed by Islamic law – but because they were afraid that any children born to Nabil, their own grandchildren bearing the Madani family name, would be brought up as Christians rather than as Muslims. That was their greatest worry, especially as they now knew that Nabil had some kind of interest in Christianity.

Nabil wrote them a short letter explaining the situation and enclosed a photo of Renata. Their response was cool. She was much too old for him (actually she was three years younger than Nabil, but in Arab eyes five years' age difference or more is preferable). It was a stupid thing for him to do – he could marry a girl from the most respectable families in Syria. What did he want a foreigner and a Christian for? Hasib and Fairouz tried hard to entice him back to Damascus and promised they would arrange a marriage for him to any girl he fancied in Syria if he would only return, but Nabil refused. He was afraid of his father's harsh manner and of the constant supervision he would be under if he ever went back to his family, and he was going to marry Renata and no other, come what may! Perceiving his determination, they then tried to get him to convert her to Islam. If she converted, they would be happy to accept her as their daughter-in-law and Nabil and

Renata would even be welcome to live with them. They were willing to do anything as long as they were assured that their grandchildren would be Muslims.

The procedures to get the marriage approved took eighteen months. The Syrian authorities required hundreds of forms and papers. They even investigated whether Renata had any Jewish blood in her. She had to provide her ancestral genealogy for several generations back and get it all translated into Arabic. All of this had to be sent to Damascus for approval, and then back to Warsaw. It was a bureaucratic nightmare! Finally Nabil had resource to his father's old trick – connections. He had a friend from high school days in Damascus who was friendly with one of the president's sons. Nabil begged him to do something as he could see no way out of the bureaucratic maze. The friend kindly obliged and mentioned Nabil's case to the president's son, who phoned someone in the appropriate ministry and all at once – everything was miraculously approved!

Hasib knew nothing about these contacts with the presidential family at the time. When he later heard about the help given by this friend, he was very upset and cut off all relationship with him. He had sincerely hoped the permits would never go through and that Nabil would return to his senses and give up his Christian girlfriend.

Finally Nabil and Renata had all the paper work sorted out and all the necessary permits, both Polish and Syrian, in their hands. They were married at a civil ceremony in Cracow in February 1986. Nabil stayed on for two months in Poland, then had to return to Dubai to continue his work. It was at that juncture that the quarrel with Ahmad flared up and Nabil was fired and decided to leave the Gulf. It was in December 1986 that Nabil left Dubai for good to join his young Polish wife in Cracow, just in time for the birth of their first boy Piotr.

Nabil had hoped he would be able to start a new life in Poland, get a job and establish himself there, but his hopes were soon dashed. There seemed to be no way of obtaining a residency permit. As a tourist he had to exchange $15 a day at the official exchange rate – it was worth much more on the black market – and even so he had to renew his visa every month and he wasn't allowed to be gainfully employed. His savings were running out fast. He tried every door he could think of – but to no avail. In desperation he contacted the Syrian embassy in Warsaw and asked them to put pressure on the Polish immigration authorities on his behalf, but they refused. The Syrian consul told him that there was no way they would interfere in an internal Polish matter – the best thing for Nabil to do was to return to Damascus.

Six months after his latest arrival in Poland they went again to the Polish immigration office to ask for a month's extension on his tourist visa, but this time he was refused. It was no good saying he was married to a Polish woman – they were adamant that he must leave Poland and he could later try to re-enter from abroad. Nabil thought this might be the viewpoint of a minor official and he tried to contact the top men in the Polish ministry of interior, but they repeated the same message: if he did not leave of his own free will, they would have to deport him.

During these harrowing days Renata was struck by Nabil's steadfast faith in Jesus. He spent much time in prayer and she was touched by the sincerity and simplicity of these prayers. No ritual, no formulas – he just poured out his heart to Jesus. She could not understand why he did not make the sign of the cross before he prayed, or recite the 'Hail Mary'; she was surprised that he as a lay person read the Bible on his own – that was only for the priests; but all the same she had to admit that he had a strong and personal faith in Jesus.

Nabil and Renata finally capitulated to the vagaries of officialdom. There was nothing more they could do about it, so they decided to fly together to Damascus and see what they could achieve from the Syrian capital. In April 1986 they boarded a plane flying to Damascus. Piotr was just four months old, and Renata was by that time pregnant with her second child. She knew nothing of the Middle East, she knew Nabil's family had rejected them both and might try to take their children, but she determined to be a faithful wife and stick to her husband through thick and thin.

10

Exiles

Nabil was very worried lest his family hear of their arrival in Damascus. He had kept in touch with his favourite sister, Amal, and through her and various friends he had heard that Anwar had turned Hasib and Fairouz against him, claiming that he had converted to Christianity and was a renegade Muslim, who deserved to be killed in accordance with Islamic law. Anwar and uncle Muhammad had even urged Hasib to contact Nabil, give him a few days to recant, and if he wouldn't, fulfil the law by having him killed in one way or another. Fairouz had strongly objected, asking them to leave Nabil alone as long as he remained abroad, to which they reluctantly agreed.

Hasib, however, was furious. Nabil had brought shame on his family's name, had deeply wounded his father's pride and had turned his back on all he, Hasib, stood for. Everyone now knew about it and gossip was rife. He was ashamed to face his colleagues at the ministry. He solemnly declared before all family members that Nabil was no longer his son, that he had taken him out of his will, and that he would try to kidnap Nabil's children if ever he had the chance, and would bring them up as real Muslims. They were all warned to cut off any contact with Nabil or face their father's wrath.

Nabil and Renata hadn't told anyone of their flight to Damascus, so as to keep it secret from the family. Renata was frantic at the thought that they might take Piotr away from her. She would have liked to meet her in-laws, but was too afraid on Piotr's account. She knew that Hasib as the grandfather could legally detain his grandson in Syria, claiming that his son had apostasised from Islam. Piotr was on her Polish passport and not on Nabil's Syrian one in case she had to leave quickly on her own. On arrival they took a taxi to the Christian quarter where they rented a room in a convent which also served as a hostel.

Nabil and Renata tried getting visas to some western country at various embassies in Damascus, but none would grant them one. Finally they went to the Cypriot embassy where the consul was very friendly and sympathetic. He listened to their story and then decided to give them a ten day visa for Cyprus, although Renata was supposed to apply for it only from Warsaw. He also gave them a letter to the Cypriot immigration authorities explaining their predicament, and advised them to apply for political asylum once in Cyprus.

They now needed exit visas from Syria, so they trudged off to the Syrian ministry of interior with some trepidation. The official asked them to fill in three separate forms. Nabil had to provide a permit from the ministry of defence, and he had to give his written approval for his wife and son to receive an exit visa. It was all very complicated, and Renata was so nervous she burst into tears at one point. Finally all passports were stamped and they could leave the building with a feeling of relief. Nabil had been afraid of meeting someone who knew his father.

Six weeks after they had arrived in Damascus everything was finally ready and they went to the airport to catch their flight to Larnaca in Cyprus. At the check-in counter their luggage was found to be overweight and they were asked to pay a large sum for it. Being very short on money, Nabil looked for a friend of his uncle's who worked at the airport and asked for his help. This man spoke to the airline officials and they let the luggage through without further trouble. However he was insistent on telling the family that he had seen Nabil – he apparently knew nothing of the problem.

Nabil later heard from Amal that he had phoned Hasib, and Hasib had been very angry. He called the family together again and said he wouldn't have let Nabil and Piotr leave Syria had he known they were in Damascus. He would have had their passports cancelled and turned Piotr into a good Muslim. He repeated that Nabil was not his son anymore, and that no one was to communicate with him. Whoever

did so would be disinherited just as he had done to
Nabil.

Once in Cyprus, Nabil and Renata went to
Limassol where they rented a small flat. Nabil
phoned Amal from there, and that was when he
heard the latest news from his family. Amal told him
that Anwar and Muhammad had been outraged at
not having caught him and his family in Damascus.
They were making plans to trace him in Cyprus, then
send an emissary to give him the customary three
days to recant as required by Shari'a law. If he
didn't, they would have him killed. Hasib seemed to
approve of this plan, but Fairouz opposed it fiercely
and said she would leave Hasib if he followed it up.
'He is not our son anymore,' she said, 'so just let him
be.' They decided to abandon their wild plans,
although Iman's diplomat husband had suggested he
get the Syrian embassy in Cyprus to deport Nabil to
Syria on some trumped-up charges.

Hasib could not forget Nabil's defection. He
vowed that he would some day get both Nabil and
Piotr back to Islam. He charged Anwar not to let
Nabil enjoy his freedom but at least to try to kidnap
the children. To Fairouz he said: 'How can I face my
colleagues at work after all this? They all know that
my son is a Christian – it is a great shame on our
family honour. I gave him everything and this is how
he repays his father.'

All this Amal related to Nabil on the phone. He
was very sad. He understood his parents and he still
loved them. He knew the terrible prejudice and
misconceptions they had about Christians and Chris-

tianity. Only God could change these hardened attitudes. He, Nabil, had better cut off all communications with them for the sake of his family's safety.

Next time he phoned Amal she asked him to be brief. Her husband was giving her trouble because of her contact with Nabil. He forbade her to phone or write to him, and warned that he would divorce her if she dared disobey him. Sadly she had to ask Nabil not to contact her anymore. The last link with his family was now severed.

Nine days after their arrival in Cyprus they went to the immigration officer in Limassol with all their documents, hoping for an extension. The officer was a big man in a uniform boasting a really large and bushy moustache who reminded Nabil of his father. Having looked at their passports and read the letter from the consul in Damascus, he jumped up in rage from his chair: 'No way,' he exclaimed, 'we are a peaceful country in a very delicate situation. We have just had our civil war between Christians and Muslims. We don't want any trouble with Syria.'

Nabil explained that he couldn't return to Syria, but the officer was adamant that he must leave Cyprus immediately the visa expired. Steve had given them the address of a Lebanese believer in Limassol named Edward. Nabil went to see him, and Edward introduced him to an American friend called Richard who was a believer too. Richard went back with Nabil to the immigration office and begged them to grant the Madanis an extension on humanitarian grounds. The stern officer agreed to give them another ten days if they would put up a cash

guarantee of C£600, which Nabil didn't have.
Richard took him to his own house and asked him to
wait a while. He slipped out to his bank and came
back and put the required amount into Nabil's hand!
Nabil was very touched – this complete stranger was
willing to give him this large amount of money on
trust!

With the money in his hand Nabil rushed back to
the immigration office and handed the bills to the
amazed officer. Finally they had the ten day extension!

What to do next was the big question. Richard,
who worked as a translator for an overseas company
in Cyprus and spoke fluent Arabic, proved very
helpful. He knew people all over the place and
started phoning around to see what could be done.
Someone suggested they see the Greek Orthodox
bishop of Limassol and ask for his help. They
obtained an audience for the next day and Richard
accompanied them there. The bishop's residence was
a very impressive place, and on meeting him they had
to kiss his hand according to approved protocol. He
was actually very friendly, listened sympathetically
to their story, and said he would do his best. There
and then he wrote a letter to the chief immigration
officer in Limassol asking him to grant the Madani
family residence in Cyprus even if it broke all the
accepted rules! They thanked his excellency profusely and left in high hopes.

Armed with this letter Nabil went back to the
immigration office at the end of their allotted time.
This time they were granted forty-five days' extension

on condition that someone in Cyprus guarantee to cover all their costs — including health expenses if necessary. Richard again proved a true friend, getting his boss to write the required letter of guarantee. The unfriendly officer couldn't believe his eyes! He had tried getting them out of the country after the first ten days, and here they still were, all set to stay on for a total of sixty-five days. They seemed to have helpers and friends all over the place — he had never seen anything like it. He was sure it was all part of some sinister political plot and assured them this was the very last possible extension he would grant them.

Nabil wasn't allowed to work in Cyprus. Their funds were getting low. Through Amal he had tried to get Anwar to transfer some of the outstanding money owed him by his former boss and from the sale of his car in Dubai — but Anwar would do nothing about it. He refused to help Nabil in any way, unless he repented and apologised, saying he deserved all the troubles he got.

Richard encouraged Nabil to try various western embassies and see if they would let him emigrate to their countries, but no one was keen on Syrians and Poles — it was a losing combination. Finally they went for an interview with the Red Cross and asked to be given the status of asylum seekers on the grounds of religious persecution. The lady in the office was sympathetic, but said their case must be referred back to Red Cross headquarters in Geneva and it would take a while before they would give their verdict.

'What about their residence status in Cyprus in the meantime?' asked Richard who had again accompanied Nabil to this office to help him with the officials involved. He was a tremendous encouragement to them during those difficult months.

'That's alright,' said the Red Cross lady. 'As soon as we accept someone's application for asylum, the immigration office has to grant them a residence permit until we get the final verdict.' She gave Nabil an official letter for immigration.

'Big moustache' at the immigration office was more upset than ever. 'You are dishonest,' he accused them, 'you are playing tricks on me.' But he had no choice but to grant them another open-ended extension until the Red Cross decision was given.

They had three months of quiet on the visa front, not having to return to the immigration office, which was a real boon. Then one day someone from the Red Cross office called to ask Nabil to pass by. He went there with Richard, and the lady sadly told them that the Red Cross Headquarters in Geneva had refused their application. Nabil was devastated.

'Why did they refuse it?' asked Richard.

'They classified this case as an internal domestic problem,' she answered, 'they won't deal with it. They only deal with cases of government persecution. Can you provide some proof of that happening to you?'

'No, I can't,' said Nabil, 'I left Syria legally. The government wasn't involved in this. It was my own family who gave me trouble.'

'Did they threaten you in any way?' asked the official.

'Yes they did,' replied Nabil, 'my sister told me that my father had decided I was a Kaffir and that Islamic law needed to be applied to me. That means death.'

'Do you have it in writing?' she asked.

'No, this was conveyed by phone.'

'Can't you ask him to put it in writing?' she persisted.

Nabil laughed, this was ridiculous! Ask his father to oblige and write him a threatening letter, just so the Red Cross could help him! What kind of world did these people live in?

'We must have written proof,' she continued sympathetically. 'Why don't you write a letter as from him and sign it yourself? No one in Geneva would notice the difference.' She was trying her best to help them.

Richard and Nabil looked at each other, then shook their heads.

'Thank you, no,' they said. 'We can't do that even if it would help.'

She looked at them, clearly frustrated. 'I'm very sorry, I only want to help you. We must have written proof.'

So that was the end of this option. The lady promised she would delay writing to the immigration office about them for ten days to give them time to check other possibilities. She wished them all the best and saw them to the door.

Two weeks later Nabil had a letter from the

Cypriot Immigration Office: 'Dear Mr Madani, The
Red Cross has informed us that your application has
been refused. You are requested to leave Cyprus
within 48 hours.'

Renata was four months pregnant at the time.
Richard had a sudden brainwave.

'I wonder if pregnant women at your stage are
allowed to fly?' he mused, 'I know a doctor at the
local hospital. Let's ask him; he might know.'

Richard phoned his friend, who advised them that
according to Cypriot law a woman more than three
months into her pregnancy was not allowed to fly!
He offered to write an appropriate letter to the
authorities. Richard and Nabil drove over to the
hospital, picked up the letter, and armed with this
new authorisation marched confidently up to their
old friend of the big moustaches.

'Mrs Madani can't fly out of Cyprus because she is
four months pregnant,' they told him. 'Here is the
medical certificate to that effect.'

He was really mad. He jumped off his chair and
swore at them in Greek. 'Mr Madani must leave,' he
shouted at them, 'Mrs Madani can stay until she's
had the baby.'

'I'm sorry you take this case so personally,' said
Richard softly, 'I suggest the case be referred to the
main office in Nicosia.'

The officer seemed relieved. He threw the file at
them and they caught a taxi to Nicosia where they
saw the top official in charge of immigration. This
time they also took a Cypriot solicitor with them, a
friend of Richard's. The official studied the file and

seemed quite sympathetic to their case. Finally he picked up the phone and called the Limassol office. 'Mr Kololombo,' he said to their old friend, 'I am sending Mr Madani back to you. You must extend his visa indefinitely until his wife has given birth.'

Mr Kololombo must have had a heart attack when he heard the order. But there was nothing he could do about it. To be spiteful he insisted on getting a medical certificate from a government-employed doctor, which their friend at the hospital speedily arranged for. Back at immigration their passports were duly stamped and for the first time since arriving in Cyprus Nabil and Renata could breathe easily and relax – they could look forward to over five months of visa-problem free living! No threat of deportation hung over their heads anymore, which gave them a wonderful feeling of freedom.

11

Struggling in Limassol

Of course there were other problems. The main one was that their money had almost totally run out. Cyprus was an expensive country to live in. They had to pay rent and for utilities and there was almost no money left for food. They got so low on funds that they could hardly buy bread or milk for Piotr. Reluctantly, they started walking the beaches at night, collecting empty bottles thrown away by the tourists: Pepsi bottles, beer bottles, and whatever they could find. Armed with plastic bags they would comb the beach every night and collect as many bottles as they could find. They would take them home, wash them and then sell them at a collection point. They got approximately 1p per bottle! If they managed to collect a hundred bottles, they had enough money for a loaf of bread and some milk.

They also had some health problems but had no money for a doctor. Piotr was suffering from malnutrition, Renata was pregnant and should have had better food and medical supervision and Nabil had a bad tooth which bothered him so much he finally extracted it himself – it was a very painful operation and he suffered from a lengthy infection of the root as a result.

Renata was very faithful to Nabil during this difficult time. She could have left him and flown back to Poland with Piotr, but she didn't even consider it. Although she wasn't happy with his beliefs and didn't understand all the bureaucratic confusion they faced, she considered it her duty to cling faithfully to her husband. This touched him deeply.

During their first months in Limassol Richard and Edward had introduced them to a group of believers in Jesus who met regularly as a fellowship in various homes for prayer and Bible study. Nabil loved going there, but Renata refused. She was still a staunch Catholic and asked Nabil to find her a Catholic Church she could attend. He faithfully walked around the streets of Limassol looking into all the many Greek orthodox churches until he finally located a small Catholic church. She was happy with that and attended there regularly.

They did have their arguments and disagreements, more so under the tremendous pressure of their uncertain existence. A few times divorce seemed to lurk around the corner, as an easy way out of their problems, but by God's grace they always re-established relationships with each other and struggled on. Nabil found solace in his prayer times when he could talk quietly to his Heavenly Father and feel

his presence. Prayer became his lifeline as all material
props had disappeared, and he realised how totally
dependent he was on God for everything. Experiencing answers to prayers strengthened his faith and
helped him to grow spiritually.

His friends at the fellowship group were also very
supportive — but he was too proud to tell them the
truth about their financial situation. He couldn't beg!
He had been brought up in a well-to-do family, he
had never had to pick up things off the road or ask a
friend for material help. He didn't know how to cope
with this new situation, but God taught him some
important lessons in humility through it all.

Renata was different. She had been brought up in
the communist system where everything was scarce
and since childhood she had been used to making the
most of every scrap. She could barter in the market
for the cheapest price, and was not averse to picking
up useful things discarded by richer people in their
rubbish bins. She even found some toys in good
condition for Piotr in this way.

One day, Edward, their good friend from the
fellowship group, called at their flat.

'Is everything okay, Nabil?' he asked, 'is there
anything you need?'

'No, no,' said Nabil, too proud to admit their
need, 'everything is fine.'

Renata burst out crying. 'He's lying,' she told
Edward, and went on to explain to him their real
situation.

Edward was astonished. 'Nabil,' he said, 'this is
not right. This isn't the way a believer behaves.

Don't be too proud to accept help from others.'
Being Lebanese himself, he could understand Nabil's
behaviour to some extent, but his western friends
couldn't. From that day on they always approached
Renata with their offers of help, and things certainly
improved.

Edward was a good friend. Nabil would often visit
him in the evening after working hours. They would
sit on the roof of Edward's house and talk about the
Bible or spend time together in prayer. Nabil had
hundreds of questions about his new faith in Jesus,
and Edward was very patient as he tried to answer
them to the best of his ability. Nabil's understanding
of the Bible grew tremendously through these quiet
conversations with his friend.

Edward also provided them with a TV set and
suggested they watch Middle East Television from
Lebanon, a Christian station broadcasting in Arabic.
Nabil drank in the daily messages. After every
sermon, the preacher would invite his audience to
join him in prayer, and Nabil would kneel down at
the sofa in their living room and join in the prayer
time. This was another source of encouragement and
teaching during these difficult days.

At the fellowship, many prayed for Renata to
come to a personal faith in Jesus. During the first
months in Limassol, she wouldn't go near this
congregation. She was adamant that she wanted
Piotr to be brought up as a good Catholic. There
were times when she forbade Nabil to read his Bible
at home. However she also realised how much he
was willing to suffer for his faith. One day she said:

'This is really stupid! Why suffer so much? Just go back to Islam and return to Syria to lead a normal life, we can't struggle on forever.'

Another evening she surprised him by joining him as he went to the fellowship for a Bible study and prayer time. 'Roberta, Edward's wife invited me to come over,' she explained, 'I'll just drink coffee with you all, but don't expect me to participate!' She sat through the study and listened intently to all that was said. She joined him again for the next two studies, and after the last one she asked Edward into the kitchen for a talk. She wept as she told him that she now wanted to believe like Nabil. What should she do? How should she go about it? He assured her that there was nothing to do, but simply to believe in Jesus and all that he had done for her. There was no rite, no ceremony. Edward prayed with her and she joyfully accepted Jesus into her life.

Back at home that evening she cried a lot and apologised to Nabil for her former attitude to his faith. It was a tremendous change, and it was wonderful to be united as a couple in their relationship to God. Renata started faithfully attending the Bible studies in the fellowship, praying and reading the Bible also on her own. Her conversion was a tremendous encouragement to them in the difficulties they were facing.

Through Richard Nabil was put in touch with a company who needed an Arabic editor to check their scientific publications that had been translated from English into Arabic. They supplied him with a word processor and allowed him to work for them from his home. During the day he helped Renata with the housework, and at night he would work on the manuscripts. They were very pleased with his work and paid him for it clandestinely. The company then decided they wanted to employ him officially, so they applied to the Cypriot ministry of interior for a work permit for Nabil. They were refused. They employed a solitictor to work on the case, who took it to the highest authority, but again it was refused. The reason given was that the Madanis, on arrival in Cyprus, had applied for political asylum (as suggested to them by the Cypriot consul in Damascus). This had obviously been a mistake, and the authorities used it as an excuse to refuse them residency status and work permits in Cyprus. It was extremely frustrating.

There were many Arab refugees in Cyprus — mainly Lebanese and Palestinians. None of them seemed to have any problem in sorting out their status and making money in Cyprus, but for some reason the authorities consistently refused it to the Madanis. They were seemingly afraid of repercussions in their relationship with the Syrian government.

In the following months Nabil went around all the western embassies in Cyprus looking for an open door to enable him to emigrate to Canada, USA, Australia or Germany. They all said that he could apply, but that the application had to be referred back to the home country for approval and that would be a long process. They couldn't help with the Cypriot authorities should they ask him to leave. The

Madanis filled out innumerable application forms, but it all came to nothing. Syrians at that time were not welcome anywhere in the West because of the terrorist connection. It just seemed hopeless.

At the fellowship Nabil was introduced to Grant and Edith, an English couple working for a Christian organisation in Cyprus. Nabil liked them very much – there was something different about them and they seemed to be really touched by his difficult situation. Grant promised he would contact his organisation which had branches in many western countries and see if they didn't need a trained accountant like Nabil in one of them – they could then maybe obtain a visa for the Madani family. Another option would be to enroll them as participants in the organisation's one year training programme which some western governments recognised as valid for granting visas to trainees from non-European countries.

A few weeks later Grant heard from his English office that they needed an accountant and would be happy to apply for Nabil and family to join them in Britain for one year as members of their training programme. The Madanis would have to apply for this one year visa in Cyprus, and the office in the UK would back their application by certifying to the Home Office that they were indeed on their accepted programme.

Nabil, Renata and Piotr, accompanied by the faithful Richard, trudged again to the British embassy, this time with a glimmer of hope. Maybe this would be the answer to their prayers, the door that would finally open for them! The British consul was quite friendly. He first interviewed Renata on her own for half an hour although her English was still rather weak. Then he spoke to Nabil:

'As you know, there are no diplomatic relations between our countries.' (It was after the Hindawi case, the man who had tried to blow up an Israeli passenger plane in Britain for the Syrian secret service, and as a result Britain had broken off diplomatic ties to Syria.) 'I advise you to go to Damascus and apply from there. How long have you been in Cyprus?'

'Eleven months,' answered Nabil.

'Oh, then you must be residents here,' said the consul without actually checking their papers. 'Okay, I will try to help you. I will send your applications to London and we will wait for their decision. If you have any friends in the UK who can endorse your application, it might help.'

They left the embassy in high spirits. Had the consul checked their passports, he would have noticed that they were still on tourist visas in Cyprus for a limited time. God must have blinded his eyes! Grant promised to get his UK branch to write to the Home Office in London and fill out all the necessary paperwork for them.

The weeks went by, and they waited for an answer. Renata's delivery time arrived and their second son was born by Caesarean section. He was a healthy boy and they called him Mark. They were thankful that mother and child were doing well and that there had been no further complications.

Two weeks after the birth two policemen turned

up at their flat with a letter from the Immigration Office in Nicosia. Their time in Cyprus was up and they were ordered to leave in forty-eight hours on pain of arrest and deportation.

This was a desperate situation. Had God brought them so far just to have their situation revert to its old pattern? What were they to do? Richard and Grant, their good friends had no answer this time. They drove them around various embassies to see if someone would grant them an entry visa, but all answered that for a Syrian six months would be necessary to process a visa application.

In despair Richard suggested: 'Let's try the Greek embassy, Nabil.'

They hurried there, it was Friday afternoon and they were just about to close the doors for the weekend. Richard in his brash American manner demanded to see the consul and they let him in. He told her the Madani saga and asked her to grant them tourist visas for Greece.

'As a Syrian, you must apply in writing and wait for it to be processed,' she said. Then, on an impulse, she asked if they had the necessary photos and fee. She stamped their passports and gave them thirty day tourist visas to Greece. Handing Nabil the passports she said: 'Mr Madani, I know nothing about you. This is the first time in my life that I have stamped a visa without first referring it to Athens for approval.'

'Thank you very much,' said Nabil, 'we will not disappoint you.'

It was a miracle! They could now officially leave for Greece. They hurried home and packed all they could take with them on the ferry. Richard drove them to Limassol port and they boarded the ship that soon after set sail for Greece.

It was the end of May 1989 and the weather was extremely hot. They were all exhausted from the tension and the running around. The baby was not yet three weeks old, and Renata was still rather weak and tired. Their money was again at a low point after having paid for the ferry tickets. But at least they had been given another chance.

12

Light at the End of the Tunnel

The ferry crossing was uneventful. They sat on deck and watched the waves go by. They couldn't buy any food as they wanted to save the little money they had left for the unknown time ahead. Renata breast-fed the baby and secretly pumped some of her breast milk into a baby bottle. She added sugar and water and gave it to Piotr who drank it happily not realising its origin! Nabil tried to keep Piotr happy by playing with him and walking him around the ship so as to give Renata time with the baby. Neither Nabil nor Renata had anything to eat during the two day crossing. Finally they arrived at Piraeus harbour completely exhausted.

Grant had asked an English believer, Linda, to meet them at the port. She had business elsewhere and couldn't get there, so she sent an American friend who didn't really know or understand their special situation, to collect them. He helped them load all their luggage into his van then asked: 'Which hotel shall I take you to?'

'To be honest with you, we cannot afford a hotel,' said Nabil. 'We really must find Linda as she is our only contact here.'

The American kindly offered to pay for their first night in the hotel, but Nabil refused. He then mentioned that at the hostel he ran there was a small spare storage room vacant that they might like to use for the time being. They gladly accepted the offer and he drove them there. It was a tiny bare room with just two iron bedsteads in it – nothing else. They stayed there for two days waiting for Linda to turn up. They had nothing to do. They walked around the neighbourhood, sat, talked, waited. The mosquito season was in full swing and they couldn't sleep at night. Finally Linda turned up and arranged for them to have a better room in the hostel.

Linda had heard from Grant that just after they had boarded the ferry he had got a message from the British embassy saying their UK visas had come through! Grant rushed to the embassy to try to get them to transfer the visa to Athens, but that couldn't be done. The visas had to be returned to London and then, if authorised, sent on to Greece from there. The consul wondered why the Madanis had left before receiving their visas.

'Were they deported from Cyprus?' he asked Grant suspiciously.

'No,' answered Grant truthfully, 'they left of their own accord.'

Grant contacted his office in Britain and urged

them to push the authorities to transfer the visas to Athens as soon as possible.

These were very frustrating days for Nabil and Renata. They had almost nothing to eat. No one knew of their predicament, and they had to watch enviously whilst the hostel staff fed their three voracious dogs with the most expensive imported canned dog food. A Canadian lady living in an adjacent room kindly gave Piotr some biscuits, but otherwise they subsisted solely on bread and water.

Every morning Nabil took a bus to the centre of Athens to visit the British embassy there and wait to see if the long awaited visas had finally arrived. On his first visit, he was taken to a separate room for a tough security check as soon as they realised he was a Syrian. They were still frightened of terrorist attacks and wouldn't take any risks. It was humiliating to be singled out of the crowds for this procedure, to pass through a special detection machine, followed by a body check and endless questions. However they soon got to know him well as he continued to turn up morning after morning patiently waiting for some sign of life from London.

The first thirty days in Greece passed and there was no sign of any visa. Would the authorities grant them an extension? What if they were deported and the visas arrived after they had left? Once again the Madanis went through the excruciating experience of being so utterly helpless. They were mere pawns in the hands of powerful government bureaucracies. They had no control whatsoever over their circumstances, and once again they had to cast themselves utterly on God's mercy and cry out to him for help. Even more than in Cyprus, they felt that God had heard their prayers and were comforted.

Linda helpfully accompanied them to the Greek immigration authority. She knew the people there as they had dealt with her own visas many times. Now she approached them and asked them to help the Madani family in their difficult situation.

'See Linda,' said the man in charge, 'I really respect you and the work you are doing in Greece, but the law says tourist visas can't be extended. They must leave the country and can then return and apply for a new one.'

Linda talked with him for a while explaining how poor they were and that they couldn't afford any tickets. Finally he gave in.

'I can offer them no more than ten extra days,' he said, 'I do this only because I know that they are waiting for a UK visa. I hope they get it during these ten days – but if they don't, don't come back to me for any extension, there is nothing more I can do.'

They thanked him profusely and returned gratefully to their simple abode. Once again Nabil fell into the accustomed routine: travel to the British embassy every morning to be there when they opened at nine o'clock, wait there patiently until they shut down for the day at one o'clock.

'Sorry, Mr Madani, no news for you today, maybe tomorrow,' the staff there would console him as they closed the doors.

The ten days ticked by. The last one was a Friday. That morning Nabil said to Renata before he left:

'Renata dear, this is our last chance. If we don't get it today you must take the boys and fly back to Poland. I will certainly be deported to Syria – who knows what awaits me there? If I stay alive I will get in touch with you somehow.'

They wept in each other's arms and he left for the bus station.

At the embassy he again sat and waited. Linda had promised to come and meet him there at noon before the embassy shut for the weekend.

Around one o'clock the consul came out of his room and said:

'Mr Madani, I'm sorry nothing has arrived so far. Have a nice weekend, maybe next week will be better.'

He had no idea it was their last day.

Nabil sat there as though turned to stone. He was in a state of shock. He put his case down on the table and wept openly. The consul was embarrassed. Then he said:

'Just a moment, I can hear the telex machine in the other room. I'll go and check.'

He went out and returned a moment later with a paper in his hand.

'Mr. Madani,' he said, 'how do you spell your name?' Nabil spelled it out for him.

'Do you have all the necessary paperwork with you?' asked the consul.

Nabil nodded, but couldn't say a word. There had been too many extreme mood swings for him in this brief period of time and he fell down in a dead faint.

The consul was very helpful. He helped him into a chair, fetched some water, and said:

'Don't worry, I'll do everything for you.'

He opened Nabil's briefcase and rummaged through the papers. He found the photos, the money for the fees and other papers he needed.

'Now Mr Madani,' he asked, 'who will meet you at the airport in London?'

Nabil couldn't utter a word, his mind was blank, he was dumbstruck. Luckily for him Linda turned up at that very moment and she was soon in charge of the situation. She gave the consul all the information necessary about the programme the Madanis would be on in Britain and about the Christian organisation running it. She gave Nabil a cold Coke to revive him and told him how happy she was that things had finally worked out for him at the very last possible moment.

'You can pick your visas up on Monday,' said the consul.

Linda came again to the rescue and explained that this was the very last possible hour to get the visas, as their Greek extension ran out this very day. Seeing she was British and very persuasive the consul gave in.

'Okay, I'll do it for you right now even though it is Friday afternoon.'

The holy weekend was violated and he kindly filled out all the forms and stamped their passports which he then handed to Nabil.

'I have given you the visas, but that is no final guarantee,' he said. 'Remember there are still no diplomatic relations between London and Damascus. The immigration authorities at Heathrow could still cause you some trouble. Good luck!'

What a relief! Nabil felt he was walking on air. Another miracle had taken place. God had intervened again at the very last moment and worked things out for them! They actually possessed a valid one year visa for Britain — it was almost more than he could take in after all the disappointments of the last weeks.

They got back to their room in the hostel and Renata looked up expectantly.

'Sorry Renata, no visas again,' said Nabil.

He never understood how he could have played this cruel joke on her at that crucial time, it must have been the excitement and exhilaration. Renata broke down in tears whilst Linda rushed in to comfort her and said:

'Oh no, Renata, he's just joking. You've got the visas.'

Renata was furious! She turned around and for the first time in their married life she smacked her husband hard across the face. It hurt, and to an Arab it was doubly painful and humiliating that a woman should dare strike her husband, it was totally unacceptable in his culture. But he accepted it penitently, knowing that he deserved it.

They rushed into the city centre to buy their flight tickets to London. The earliest possible flight was on Monday, but seeing they had the visas to Britain the Greek authorities kindly agreed to let them stay on for the weekend.

On Monday morning Linda drove them out to the airport and they happily boarded the plane to London. Renata was so happy she slept the whole length of the flight. Whilst Piotr played and Mark cried, Nabil sat and prayed almost the whole three hours from Athens to London.

'Oh God, let us get through immigration this time. Surely you didn't bring us this far to let us down.'

The plane landed at Heathrow airport and they went into the terminal, picked up their luggage and headed for the passport checkpoints.

'Mr Madani,' said the lady officer, 'I see you got your visa in Greece, why not in Damascus?'

Nabil tried to appear calm and nonchalant as he explained that they had been touring around Cyprus and Greece for several months. She seemed satisfied.

'You are on a one year Christian training programme, are you not?' she continued.

Nabil affirmed that was so.

'That's interesting,' she said, 'how come your name is Nabil Muhammad?'

Nabil quietly explained that he was a Christian now.

'What are your plans when the year is over?' she queried.

'I'm sorry, but I really don't know,' answered Nabil.

'Excuse me, I have to refer this to the main officer in charge,' she said and disappeared.

Nabil felt his knees buckle. 'This is it, Renata,' he said, 'we are finished.'

The lady reappeared in a short while smiling. 'I

have a problem,' she said, 'you are Syrian and your
wife is Polish. It is unusual, I'm not sure I know
which stamp to use.'

'Put on any stamp you like,' said Nabil with a sigh
of relief.

'Here it is,' she said, handing them their passports.
'We'll contact you later. Welcome to Britain!'

God had answered their prayers and they had
succeeded! Nabil could hardly believe it was happening as with no more fuss they moved to the exit
where a member of the organisation was waiting
with a van to take them into London. A small house
had been set aside for them and they could finally
relax and breathe freely. No Damocles sword of visa
extensions and deportations hung over them now —
they had a whole year of security ahead of them!

Nabil started work as an accountant for the
organisation one week after their arrival in London.
There was much he had to get used to, such as
accounting in English. He had always worked in
Arabic before and needed to learn all the English
terms of his profession. The people in charge
however were very friendly and helped as much as
they could.

It was much more difficult for Renata to adapt, as
she had to stay with the children at home whilst
Nabil was away at work. She didn't know anyone in
the neighbourhood and her English was still rather
inadequate, so she had practically no adult company
until Nabil returned home in the evening. It was very
frustrating for her, as she then wanted to go out and
see things whilst he was exhausted from his long day

in the office. In some ways it was the most difficult year in their married life as they had to get used to 'normal' life again whilst at the same time adapting to a new language and culture. Although the believers at work and in the Church they attended were friendly, there was no real family with whom they could share their feelings and on whose shoulders they could cry. They had to cope with all the many new things on their own, sometimes with disastrous results.

They both enrolled in English courses to improve their communication with those around them. The one thing they most enjoyed was the sense of security they now possessed, so different from those tense months in Cyprus and Greece. The officials were more helpful and relaxed – even at the Home Office. Things could be dealt with by letter, there was no hassle, and there was no desperate running to Government offices. You were treated as a human being with dignity and rights – so different from the Middle East scene where bureaucrats assume they are little gods and treat regular citizens as scum. It was a taste of paradise!

Of course they suffered a certain amount of culture shock in the UK. After the gregariousness of the Middle East and Poland, British people seemed so uncommunicative, private and stiff. There was no sharing of personal problems, no dropping in on people unawares for a visit and a leisurely chat – and no one visited them. It took them a while to realise people were actually quite friendly and concerned for them even though they didn't express it in words. In

Syria Nabil had been accustomed to visitors dropping in at any time of the day for a chat, or the
family going out to visit other family and friends —
you were never alone, you were always with people,
talking, sharing or gossiping. In London they learned
to sit alone inside their own four walls day after day
knowing no one would drop in for a visit, yet hoping
the miracle would happen and someone would turn
up after all. They were so lonely, it was difficult to
get used to this way of life.

Later that year the organisation offices were moved
to a smaller town in the Northwest of England, and
the Madanis moved with them. Here they slowly
settled into a normal lifestyle, finding a church where
they were gladly accepted and helped. It was the first
time in their married life that they had a settled
home, a stable job situation, a friendly church where
they got to know people on a personal basis. They
really enjoyed this feeling of stability.

Another source of joy was that Renata's mother
could now freely come to visit them and her dear
grandchildren in England. The breakdown of the
communist regimes in eastern Europe has made such
visits easier.

Of course there was the annual visa problem.
Would they be allowed to stay on in Britain
for another year? How long could they stay on?
What if . . .?

At the end of their first year the Home Office
granted them an extension for another year. That
was great. The second year went by, and again fears
and doubts raised their ugly heads. Their vicar

suggested they apply for political asylum in Britain. He knew the local MP and arranged for an interview with him. The MP was impressed by their situation and promised to help as best he could. He wrote on their behalf to the Home Office, who then contacted the Madanis and sent them many forms to fill out. They did so, and sent them in as an official application for asylum in April 1991. Today they are still waiting for the final decision on their application, and trust God will finally answer their prayers and grant them the right to live permanently in their adoptive country where they are putting down roots. They cannot imagine being uprooted again and it is still difficult for them to come to terms with the constant uncertainty until their case is finalised.

However, one lesson they have learnt through their long saga is that they can trust God to answer prayer and to see them through. Their faith has been tested many times during the ups and downs of their asylum hunting. The extra pressures have at times seemed almost unbearable, yet God always intervened and provided for them. Their ultimate security is now in him, not in connections and in high-placed officials. Through faith in Christ they have found a personal God with whom they can have a direct relationship, a loving father who cares and intervenes on behalf of his children in the affairs of this world. No, it wasn't all rosy and cosy – there were struggles and failures, but they can testify that faith works, prayer works, God works in them and for them.

Above all they know that in Christ their sins are forgiven and they are assured of a place in Heaven. They have peace with God and peace within their souls. This is their real security, and the problems of this life fade into insignificance when compared with it.

From the unknown God of Islam and the remote God of Catholicism, they have come to accept and to know Christ as their personal Saviour and Lord, and through him they have developed a deep personal relationship to God. This is their most prized possession. They wouldn't go back to their former religious systems for anything. They have advanced from shadows to reality, from legalistic rituals to the real inner substance, from working hard to earn merit with a seemingly capricious God to the security of being 'in Christ' — sheltered and covered by his blood and righteousness, indwelt by his Spirit.

Like Paul the apostle they can now say: 'Forgetting what is behind and straining towards what is ahead, I press on towards the goal to win the prize for which God has called me heavenwards in Christ Jesus' (Phil 3:13,14).

Nabil and Renata are firm believers in the power of prayer. Their greatest desire is for a reconciliation with the family in Syria. They pray for it regularly and fervently, and wait expectantly, certain that the God who has led them thus far will work this out for them too. They would love to return to Syria and live there if at all possible. Nabil longs for his own country and people and realises the many good things in Middle Eastern culture as compared with the West. He still feels himself to be a loyal Syrian Arab, proud of his history and civilisation. Faith in Christ has given him a greater love for his nation and a greater sense of identity with them. Jesus was born and grew up in a Middle Eastern society, so it is actually much easier for people from the Middle East to understand his parables and stories, to grasp his teaching. Nabil is sure that God will open many eyes in that area of the world to the same truth that was revealed to him by God's grace.

There is no bitterness in the hearts of Nabil and Renata towards anyone, only love and forgiveness which Christ himself places within them as they seek to follow his supreme example along the narrow road that leads to eternal life.

Postscript

As this book goes into print, Nabil and Renata are still waiting for the final word from the British Home Office. Whatever the outcome, they feel secure in the hands of the Messiah who loved them and gave himself for them. Their prayer is that this book may be a guide to other Muslims who are searching for the right path to God, a link in a chain of events and insights that will lead the true seekers to the only source of life, love, knowledge and salvation.

You too can discover that Jesus, the Messiah, is the only true path to God. You too can discover that his sacrifice for your sins gives you forgiveness and peace with God.

All alone in the privacy of your home or any other place you may be in, you can turn directly to God and simply say to him: 'I believe that the Messiah is the true path to you, I believe that his sacrifice atones

for my sins, I accept him into my heart and I thank
you that he has done everything needed to give me
peace with you.'

God does not enter our lives by force. He prepares
the circumstances and then knocks on the doors of
our hearts. Everyone ought to respond to God's
initiative and accept his way of forgiving sins. When
you do this, you too will receive the gift of new life
from him.

God has promised to receive everyone who comes
to him in this simple way. He will receive you as you
are and will then change you from within. He will
forgive your sins, cleanse you and give you power to
live in joy and peace in this troubled world.

Having put your trust in Jesus the Messiah, you
must now develop your faith and your spiritual life:

1. Read God's Word, the Bible, regularly – it is
your spiritual food.

2. Pray to God through the Messiah in simple
and spontaneous words. No formulas are needed.
This is your personal link with God. Pour out your
heart to him, silence your heart before him and listen
to his voice.

3. Find friends with similar beliefs. You need
their encouragement and support.

4. Talk to others about your faith – they also
need to discover the true path for themselves.

Glossary

'Alawis—A Muslim sect, living mainly in northwestern Syria. Considered heretical by the orthodox Sunni majority.

Aramaic— Ancient Semitic language that was prevalent all over the Middle East until supplanted by Arabic. Also called Syriac, it is the liturgical language of some ancient eastern churches.

Assassins—an extreme branch of the Isma'ili Muslim sect, that established itself in the mountains of the Levant around the era of the Crusades. It was notorious for assassinating its enemies.

Baraka—Divine blessing, grace and power residing in a saint. It is believed that it can be passed on to others by touch.

Caliphs—Leaders of the Muslim world after Muhammad's death.

Druze—An offshoot of the Isma'ili sect, now forming an independent religion, living mainly in Syria, Lebanon and Israel, and considered heretical by the Sunni majority.

Fatwa—Religious edict or decision on a controversial question issued by a Muslim judge.

Fiqh—The science of Islamic law. The Islamic jurist's understanding of the Shari'ah acquired through pious scholarship.

Hadith—The collection of Muhammad's sayings and doings considered binding on all Muslims in matters of faith and practice.

Haj—The pilgrimage to Mecca, one of the five pillars of Islam, binding on all Muslims who are fit and can afford it.

Hejirah—Muhammad's flight from Mecca to Medinah. The Islamic calendar is dated from that day.

Ihram—The special white cotton garment donned by the pilgrims at the start of the pilgrimage.

Injil—Arabic word for the Gospels, also used of the whole New Testament.

Issa—Arabic Islamic name for Jesus. Christian Arabs use the name Yassu'.

Isma'ilis—an extreme Shi'a sect that branched off from the main group after a controversy over the succession to the sixth Imam. Was very powerful between the 9th and the 12th centuries.

Jacobite Church—The ancient Syrian Orthodox monophysite (non-Chalcedonian) church.

Jebel—Arabic for mountain.

Ka'abah—The cube like building at the centre of the great mosque of Mecca, contains the holy black stone. Centre of Muslim veneration and pilgrimage.

Kaffir—Unbeliever, heathen, also used of an apostate Muslim.

Madhab—A Sunni school of thought and commentary. There are four such officially-recognised schools.

Maryam—Arabic name for Mary.

Matta—Arabic for Matthew.

Melkite—Name applied to the Greek–Catholic uniate church in the Middle East.

Muezzin—The man whose duty it is to call the faithful to prayer five times a day from the minaret.

Qur'an—The Holy Book of Islam containing 114 chapters (suras). Claimed to have been revealed to Muhammad by the angel Gabriel.

Ramadan—The Muslim month of fasting. All Muslims are to abstain totally from food, drink, sex and tobacco from dawn to sunset.

Salat—The daily prayers in Islam, performed five times: at dawn, noon, afternoon, sunset, and before sleeping.

Shafi'i—One of the four schools (madhabs) of Sunni Islam.

Shahadah—The profession of faith: 'There is no God but Allah and Muhammad is the messenger of Allah.' It is the first Pillar of Islam.

Shari'a—The total body of Islamic law binding on all believers. It has four sources: Qur'an, Hadith, Ijma' (consensus) and Qiyas (analogical deduction).

Shi'a—Branch of Islam that accepts only 'Ali (Muhammad's son-in-law) and his descendants as true leaders of the Muslim world.

Shirk—Ascribing a partner to God. Worst sin in Muslim eyes. Christians are accused of committing it by claiming Jesus is divine.

Sufi—Muslim mystic, follower of one of the orders of Sufism.

Sunnah—Main branch of Islam that accepts the historical first Caliphs as authentic leaders of Islam after Muhammad's death. Sunnah is also the compilation of Muhammad's sayings and way of life, a source of Islamic law.

Suweida—Capital of the Jebel a-Druze area (today renamed Jebel al-'Arab) in southern Syria.

Syriac—Aramaic of the first centuries after Christ as used by the ancient eastern churches.

Tawrah—Arabic for the Pentateuch, the law given to Moses.

Umayads—The first dynasty of Caliphs that ruled the Muslim empire from their capital of Damascus. Founded by Mu'awiya in the 7th century.

Ummah—The whole Muslim world seen as one united community of faith.

Wahabbi—Member of a puritan renewal sect originating in Arabia in the 18th century. Founded by 'Abd al-Wahab. Wahabbism is the official creed of Saudi Arabia.

Zabur—Islamic Arabic for the Psalms of David.

Zakat—Almsgiving, the tax incumbent on all Muslims and distributed to the poor. One of the five pillars of Islam.